D1566594

RUTHERFORD

RECOLLECTIONS OF THE CAMBRIDGE DAYS

ISBN 0-444-40968-8

RUTHERFORD — RECOLLECTIONS OF THE CAMBRIDGE DAYS

by **Mark Oliphant,**

Government House, Adelaide; formerly Research School of the Physical Sciences, The Australian National University, Canberra.

The author, one of the very few who worked closely with Lord Rutherford, and who knew him and Lady Rutherford personally, records here his recollections of Rutherford at home, on holiday and in the laboratory, together with such memories of this great man of science as he has been able to obtain from contemporaries, colleagues and students.

The Foreword, written by Sir James Chadwick, gives additional insight into the character and achievements of Lord Rutherford.

Mark Oliphant was born in 1901 in South Australia where he attended Unley and Adelaide high schools and the University of Adelaide. He migrated to Britain in 1927 to work as a research student with Rutherford in the Cavendish Laboratory, Cambridge, and remained there for 10 years. Subsequently he was Professor of Physics at the University of Birmingham and spent the war years working on radar in England and the United States of America. In 1950 he returned to Australia to the newly created National University in Canberra as Director of its Research School of Physical Sciences. Appointment as Governor of South Australia followed in 1971.

He is a Fellow of the Royal Society of London and was the first President of the Australian Academy of Science. He has travelled widely and has been much concerned with the problems of the place of science and of scientists in society.

R Schwabe
1928

RUTHERFORD
RECOLLECTIONS OF THE
CAMBRIDGE DAYS

by

MARK OLIPHANT

Government House, Adelaide

ELSEVIER PUBLISHING COMPANY

AMSTERDAM LONDON NEW YORK

1972

ELSEVIER PUBLISHING COMPANY
335 JAN VAN GALENSTRAAT
P.O. BOX 211, AMSTERDAM, THE NETHERLANDS

AMERICAN ELSEVIER PUBLISHING COMPANY, INC.
52 VANDERBILT AVENUE
NEW YORK, NEW YORK 10017

LIBRARY OF CONGRESS CARD NUMBER: 70-180066
ISBN 0-444-40968-8
WITH 37 ILLUSTRATIONS

PRINTED IN THE NETHERLANDS

For Michael

Rutherford
Recollections of the Cambridge Days
BY MARK OLIPHANT

Foreword

I have read this book of recollections of Rutherford in Cambridge by my friend Sir Mark Oliphant with deep pleasure, for it is written by one who not only had almost daily contact with Rutherford in the Cavendish Laboratory for the last 10 years of Rutherford's life but who, with his wife Rose, was a welcome and frequent visitor to the Rutherfords at their home and who spent many vacations with them in their country cottage. Thus the reader gets a picture of Rutherford as a man as well as a scientist by one who had a deep affection for him and whose affection was returned. The personal relations between Rutherford and Mark Oliphant were, in the latter years, akin to those between father and son. This intimate relation is not emphasized but appears almost casually; and it does not cloud the author's judgement of Rutherford as a man or prevent him from mentioning occasional instances of temper or of unreasonableness, which were almost always quickly repaired.

In his Introduction Sir Mark mentions Rutherford's early years in New Zealand very briefly, for much has been written about his family background, and about his progress from primary school to Nelson College, where he received the mental stimulus he needed from two able schoolmasters, for which he was deeply grateful to the end of his life; and thence to Canterbury University College where, in his fifth year, he began to concentrate on science.

With little guidance and with the most meagre facilities he produced some remarkable and original work, especially on the detection of Hertzian waves.

It was, however, only by a quirk of fate that Rutherford was awarded an 1851 Exhibition Scholarship. This enabled him to come to England and to enter, in October 1895, the Cavendish Laboratory under J. J. Thomson as an "advanced student". There he continued his work on Hertzian waves with such success that he became known personally to many of the senior members of the University. All who met him were impressed by his unusual ability. After only two terms in the Cavendish he was invited by J.J. to work with him on the ionization of gases produced by the newly discovered Röntgen rays. This work, satisfactorily concluded, led Rutherford to examine the radiation from uranium, another recent discovery by Becquerel, by the ionization methods he had worked out. This started him on his extraordinary work on radio-activity at McGill University, Montreal, where he had been elected Macdonald Professor of Physics in 1898. He was fortunate to have there John Cox as Head of the Physics Department. John Cox, with William Peterson, Principal of McGill, had interviewed Rutherford in Cambridge and had formed the highest regard for his ability. He shielded Rutherford as far as possible from burdens which would interfere with his research work and so set him free to devote his energy to the study of radio-activity. This culminated in the revolutionary theory put forward by Rutherford and Soddy, a junior demonstrator in the Chemistry Department who had joined Rutherford to help with the chemical aspects, that radioactivity was a spontaneous disintegration of the atom, in which one kind of matter changes into another kind having different chemical and radioactive properties, with the simultaneous emission of energy in the form of radiation. This startling theory, though supported by experiment, albeit on quantities of matter so minute that they could not be detected except by their radiations, was anathema to some of his colleagues at McGill. It is related by A. Norman Shaw that some senior colleagues begged him not to publish the theory, in the fear that it would bring discredit on McGill. But he was supported by others and particularly by John Cox who, in the words of Norman Shaw, "ventured also to predict that some day Rutherford's experimental work would be rated as the greatest since that of Faraday".

The disintegration theory seems to have created little interest or understanding except in England, though even there there were some who were sceptical at first. It is much to the credit of the Council of the Royal Society that Rutherford was elected a Fellow of the Society in 1903, invited to give the Bakerian Lecture in 1904, and awarded the Rumford Medal in 1905; an unmistakable recognition of his genius.

Among those who were deeply impressed by Rutherford was Arthur Schuster, Professor of Physics in Manchester; and he it was who persuaded Rutherford to return to this country in 1907, by offering to resign the Chair in his favour. Schuster did much to help Rutherford for, with the perception and generosity characteristic of so many of his race, he persuaded the University to establish a Readership in Mathematical Physics, for which he paid the stipend for some years; and later he enabled Rutherford to retain the services of Hans Geiger as Research Assistant, Schuster again providing the stipend.

Rutherford's remarkable work in Manchester was made possible by the personal loan to him of some 250 mgm. of radium by the Vienna Academy of Sciences. After the war, when he had taken this radium with him to Cambridge, he resisted attempts to confiscate it as enemy property and arranged for its purchase, an act which rescued the Radiuminstitut of Vienna from dire poverty and which earned for him the life-long gratitude of its Director, Stefan Meyer.

In Manchester he made, among much other work of great importance, two outstanding contributions – the first being the theory of the nuclear atom, a revolution in our understanding of the structure of matter, and the second the discovery that the nitrogen nucleus could be disintegrated by the impact of α-particles.

Shortly after Rutherford had reluctantly decided to move to Cambridge to succeed his former teacher, J. J. Thomson, he asked me to go there to help to get work started, and he helped to make it possible. Even in my early years as a research student he would sometimes consult me about the direction the laboratory should take. I remember well that he would often say "I have done enough for one man; it is now the task of the younger generation to tackle the problems about the structure of the nucleus". It was obvious that he had to lead us. So it came about that the main line of attack of the Cavendish was on problems connected, directly or indirectly, with the atomic nucleus. This was perhaps the first time that a great laboratory had concentrated so large a part of its effort on one particular problem.

Another aspect of the Cavendish was the high proportion of students from the Commonwealth. It was natural that Commonwealth students would wish to work under one of the greatest experimental scientists, himself from the Commonwealth. Thus it was that in some years there would be as may as 9 or 10 such students, a quarter to a third of the total number. They were a great asset to the laboratory. Sir Mark himself was one of them.

Sir Mark makes evident the attention which Rutherford devoted to his research students and his ability to inspire them, thus creating a lively and happy community. They were sometimes hampered by the lack of equipment, for Rutherford's one defect was that he would not ask for money to provide material facilities or technical staff. In my view, much more could have been accomplished in the Cavendish if Rutherford had not been so modest in his demands.

In his later years Rutherford began to take much interest in the relations between new discoveries in science and their application in industry. This is very clear from the author's quotation from his Norman Lockyer Lecture of 1936, in which Rutherford advocated the setting up by the Government of a "Prevision Committee", which would advise about the probable effects of new inventions in industry and their possible influence on the distribution of labour and capital. It is a calamity that Rutherford died so early, before he could use his growing public influence to spread his ideas more widely and to press for their adoption.

As the author so clearly brings out, Rutherford was never so fully relaxed as when he was in the countryside. He was at heart still a countryman as he had been in his youth. I remember a walk with him on the Yorkshire moors, in the early 1920's, when he maintained that an active family should, every few years, leave the town and live in the country. When I pointed out the difficulties he compromised that perhaps a long stay in the country every year might suffice. His point was partly that one should get away from the tensions of urban life and so recharge one's batteries but chiefly that one needed to regain contact with nature and the country life on which man ultimately depends. In this view, if in few others, he would have agreed with Virginia Woolf when she wrote "The peasants are the great sanctuary of sanity, the country the last stronghold of happiness".

I like to think that in the omnivorous reading of his latter days – biographies, historical works, war campaigns – he included some of the works of Thomas Hardy, our great novelist of country life, for I shall end this foreword by a quotation of part of the last paragraph of "The Woodlanders": – "If I ever forget your name let me forget home and heaven. . . . . I never can forget 'ee; for you was a good man, and did good things".

All over the world Rutherford is recognized as one of the greatest scientists of all time; but to the many men who worked with and under him, to whom he would often refer, with some affection and perhaps a touch of arrogance, as "my boys" he is remembered as a great man and a good man, who did good things.

J. Chadwick

Preface

I thank all who have contributed recollections, anecdotes, illustrations or facts for use in this book, especially E. T. S. Walton, P. I. Dee, E. Bretscher, A. E. Kempton, P. Kapitza, W. B. Lewis, P. Fowler, and many others with whom I have discussed this project. I owe a great debt to Sir James Chadwick, who has read the manuscript and corrected many errors of fact and expression, and who contributed largely to its contents. My thanks are due to the Cambridge University Press for permission to use extracts from the official biography of Rutherford by A. S. Eve; to those who, over the years contributed to my snapshot album; to my wife, and my son Michael, who read the typescript with a critical eye; and above all, to Lord and Lady Rutherford, who gave so generously of their affection throughout the period 1927–1937.

Finally, I express my gratitude to the Ian Potter Foundation which provided secretarial assistance by Miss Mackie when it was most needed.

Contents

Introduction

"I fear that you are right in saying that very few men indeed are interested in Rutherford's work. I suppose that to a young man of the present day it all looks so easy and so obvious."

This quotation from a letter written to me by Sir James Chadwick expresses clearly why I feel it necessary to put on record my own recollections of one who must rank with the very greatest in natural science, and to record and bring together those of as many others as possible. There is growing interest in the attempt to understand how new concepts are generated, and the history of ideas is becoming an increasingly important discipline. However, analysis of published papers and books on physics gives little information about those who wrote them, other than of their status as men of science, though their personalities, their relations with their colleagues, and their techniques of inspiration of others, are of equal importance.

Sir Henry Tizard, for whom Rutherford had a great affection, in his Rutherford Memorial Lecture[1] before the Chemical Society, delivered in the Royal Institution on 29th March, 1939, contrasted Rutherford with Dr. Johnson:

"I have heard it said that it was a pity that Rutherford had no Boswell, that no one of the many men who worked in daily contact with him made notes on his

1

ways, of his sayings, of his few mistakes as well as his many successes, of his manners, good and bad, and of his faults as well as of his virtues. I share the feeling. His name will live for ever in the history of science, and yet one would like to feel that Rutherford himself lived in the history of our times as no man of science has ever lived before. In many ways Rutherford was indeed very like the great Dr. Johnson. He came to dominate the scientific world of his time in exactly the same way as Johnson had dominated the literary world. Like Johnson he had occasional sallies of heat of temper and at times of passionate unreasonableness. He was the centre of attraction at any scientific gathering, and especially at the dinners of the Royal Society Club where some of us used to hang about in the hopes of hearing him say, 'come and sit by me.' Then just as people were always a little frightened of Johnson so I think we were a bit frightened of Rutherford, not because he could or would do us any harm but because we might fall short of his own standard of work and conduct. Of course, the shortcomings were there, but we preferred him not to observe them. Like Johnson, too, he never considered whether he should be a grave man or a merry man, but just let inclination for the time take its course. He had a boisterous sense of fun and a loud laugh. By precept and by example he helped to keep our minds free from cant. He hated pomposity and artificiality. He loved simple people, and simple ways, and lived a simple life. He brushed little annoyances aside.

But in other respects he was very unlike Johnson. Poor Dr. Johnson suffered from ill health all his life, and was subject to severe fits of depression. So if we can find similarities we can also find great contrasts. Johnson lived on the whole a life of laziness interrupted by periods of feverish activity to which he was driven by

2

lack of money. Rutherford was at the top of his form at breakfast,* a thing that weaker men affect to despise, and lived a life of feverish intellectual activity relieved by short periods of magnificent idleness. When he took a holiday it really was a holiday.

There is another curious contrast with Johnson. Whereas Dr. Johnson used to relieve his literary labours by doing chemical experiments and by talking science, so Rutherford used to relieve his scientific labours by a study of literature. In his early days he was a great novel reader. When he was at Montreal, working long hours in the laboratory, the librarian found it difficult to supply him with enough light literature for his leisure moments. But later on in life he gave up the reading of novels or any form of imaginative literature, and confined himself to history and biography, to books that dealt with facts. I think he must have surprised many people from time to time by his knowledge of ancient history. He had a retentive memory, and an absurdly entertaining way of burlesquing hackneyed quotations or common proverbs, as for instance on one occasion when we were discussing short-lived reputations of men who rashly announced discoveries which were soon detected as false, he said: 'Well, 'tis better to have boomed and bust than never to have boomed at all'.''

The sophistication of modern physics, particularly the theoretical aspects of the structure of matter, conceals the deep and often expressed conviction of Rutherford, and of his disciple and colleague Niels Bohr, that nature is essentially simple. Both felt that understanding could not be wrapped up in obscurity, or be expressed only in highly

* Sometimes! More often silent and taciturn, and occasionally downright bad tempered. News of his mood when he arrived in his office spread rapidly among members of the Laboratory.

technical jargon. Rutherford's love of the alpha-particle, of the nucleus and the particles from which it is built, was deep and personal. He identified himself with the sub-microscopic world in which he worked as completely as an historian with the people whose lives and times he uncovers. For him, the scientific life was a tremendous adventure, and not just an exercise of intellect.

In what follows there is a very brief account of Rutherford's life, from his birth to 1919, when he left Manchester for the Cavendish Laboratory, followed by recollections of the Cambridge period, personal and otherwise, which I have been able to put together. It should be regarded as a supplement to Eve's official biography[2], rather than another life of Rutherford.

1871–1919

Ernest Rutherford was born in New Zealand on 30th August, 1871, the second son and fourth child in a large family of twelve children. His grandfather had migrated from Scotland to New Zealand in 1842, when his father, James, was three years of age. James followed his father's trade as a wheelwright. He met and married Martha Thomson and settled near Nelson, in the South Island, on a small farm. When Ernest was eleven years of age, the family moved to Havelock, a short distance away, where his father established a mill to treat the native flax of the area, and a small sawmill. Ernest did well at the primary school and at fifteen won a scholarship to Nelson College. His school education was broad, for he distinguished himself in Latin, French, English Literature, History, Physics and Chemistry, becoming Head of the School. He played games reasonably well and entered fully into the non-academic life of the school. He took photographs with a home-made came-

4

ra, dismembered clocks and made models of the water wheels which his father used to obtain power for his mills. Under the influence of his fine mother and his teachers, Rutherford developed a wide tast for literature, and read avidly and omnivorously all his life.

In 1889, he won a scholarship to Canterbury College, Christchurch, a component of the University of New Zealand where, as one of only 150 students in a small institution, he enjoyed five very full years. He obtained his B.A. degree in Latin, English, French, Mathematics, Mechanics and Physical Science, and the M.A. degree, after four years, with a double first in Mathematics and Physical Science.

During his fifth year in Canterbury College, Rutherford concentrated on science, carrying out many experiments on the electromagnetic waves discovered by Hertz, and investigating the effects of the damped oscillations of the Hertzian oscillator upon the magnetization of steel needles and iron wires. Ingeniously, he showed that the magnetization was confined to a thin, outer layer of the metal, by etching away the surface with acid. He used these magnetic effects to detect wireless waves at a distance from his oscillator, even through brick walls.

Rutherford reproduced Tesla's experiments on the high voltages which could be obtained from a resonant transformer, and developed methods for measuring intervals of time as small as ten microseconds. He lectured to meetings of the Science Society on his work, and on the evolution of the chemical elements, and published two papers in the Transactions of the New Zealand Institute. His first experience of teaching came from the necessity to supplement his scholarship by coaching students. To save money, he went to live with a widow, Mrs. de Renzi Newton, whose daughter, Mary, he married later.

In 1895 Rutherford applied for an 1851 Scholarship,

which was awarded in alternate years to a New Zealand student in science. The Commissioners, in London, awarded this to MacLaurin, a chemist, but they had before them a recommendation from their assessors that a second scholarship be awarded to Rutherford, action which they were unable to take. However, MacLaurin decided to accept a post in the Civil Service, so the award was transferred to Rutherford. So, the fates conspired to enable this young New Zealander to go to Cambridge to work with J.J. Thomson.

Rutherford had to borrow the money to pay for his passage to England. He entered Trinity College in 1895, to become the first of the new category of research students, J.S. Townsend, of gas discharge fame, entering almost simultaneously. He settled quickly into the Cavendish Laboratory, where J.J. Thomson approved of his desire to carry further his experiments on the detection of electromagnetic waves by use of the effects of high frequency currents upon the magnetization of iron wires. He was ambitious, and thought that he might make his fortune from his detection of wireless signals so that he could marry Mary Newton. Before Marconi, he detected radio waves half a mile from the transmitter, and ultimately over the two miles between the Cavendish and the University Observatory.

At this time, two major discoveries were made of completely new physical phenomena. These were the observations of X-rays by Roentgen, and of radioactivity, by Becquerel, and each opened up hitherto unsuspected areas of investigation which were destined to change the course of physics and chemistry. J.J. Thomson, who wished to use the ionizing effect of X-rays in his investigations of electricity in gases, invited Rutherford to join him. Rutherford, who had developed early an extraordinary ability to recognize, and concentrate upon the puzzling frontier problems of physics, seized the opportunity to move into more exciting fundamental studies with a scientist of Thomson's experience and reputation.

Rutherford showed that the ionizing effect of X-rays was due to the production of positive and negative ions in equal numbers, and he devised ingenious methods for measuring the velocity of drift of these ions in an electric field. In 1898 he investigated the ions produced when ultraviolet light fell on a metal plate, showing that they were all negative ions produced at or near the metal plate, and that their properties were identical with those of ions produced by X-rays. When he heard that the radiations which Becquerel had found to be emitted spontaneously by uranium were able to ionize gases, Rutherford investigated the ions produced and found them to be identical with those with which he had already worked. He showed that there were two kinds of radiation producing ionization, an easily observable and strongly ionizing component which he called alpha-rays, and a more penetrating component to which he gave the name beta-rays. Rutherford had found the field of physics in which he was to spend his life.

In August 1898, Rutherford was appointed to the Macdonald Research Professorship of Physics at McGill University, Montreal, Canada. He was only 27 years of age and had applied for the post with reluctance after assessing his prospects in Cambridge, mostly because he wished to marry. Having made the decision, he set to work at McGill on further studies of radioactivity, with unabated enthusiasm. In the summer of 1900 he went to New Zealand to collect his bride, returning to McGill in the autumn. In 1901 their only child, a daughter, Eileen, was born.

The fascinating story of Rutherford's researches at

McGill is to be found in detail elsewhere*. A group of research workers soon gathered round him, and together, like a band of detectives, they unravelled the complex series of radioactive disintegrations of thorium and of radium, showing that both end as stable isotopes of lead. The chemist, Soddy, allied himself with Rutherford in this important work, while the now celebrated German chemist, Otto Hahn, who was to discover nuclear fission in 1938, became a research student. Professor Hahn, in a tribute to his revered master, wrote in 1937[3]:

"Early in the year 1906, a photographer came to the Macdonald Physics Building to take a photograph of Rutherford working in his laboratory, for publication in the columns of 'Nature' with an article by Dr. A. S. Eve on the Macdonald Physics Building. Rutherford was at first reluctant, but later he granted the photographer permission to take a few flash-light photographs showing him seated at his α-ray apparatus. The photographs were duly taken, and they were also quite good. In the opinion of the photographer, however, the already famous professor was not dressed elegantly enough for the readers of 'Nature'. Not even cuffs were to be seen peeping from the sleeves of his coat! But the photographer found a way out; I was to lend Rutherford my loose cuffs. They were so arranged that they protruded well beyond the end of his sleeves. The photographer expressed satisfaction with the new photograph. As a result, in one of the volumes of 'Nature' for the year 1906 ('Nature', vol. 74, p. 273) we see not only Prof. Rutherford seated alongside the apparatus with which he carried out his epoch-making experiments on the α-rays, but also one of the cuffs of a young research student, who treasures his sojourn with one of the greatest masters of

* A.S. Eve, loc. cit.

8

physical research as one of the most beautiful memories of his life."

In Montreal, Rutherford demonstrated his unique capacity to inspire others, while himself carrying out work of great significance, alone and with collaborators of all ages. Apart from showing that radioactivity was a property of atoms, and independent of all other physical and chemical properties, and that the emission of an alpha-particle carrying two elementary charges of electricity of positive sign, or of a beta-particle which is a negative electron, transformed the atom from one chemical species to another, Rutherford and his co-workers showed that the high output of energy "is derived from the latent energy in the radium atoms and is released in the successive stages of their disintegration." He showed that the alpha-particles were probably helium atoms with electric charge $+2e$, with velocity equal to nearly one-tenth of the velocity of light.

Writing of his eminent pupil[4], J.J. Thomson said:

"Rutherford's scientific activity was never greater than when he was at Montreal... In those days, laboratories had no funds to buy instruments as sensitive as those now available, and the detection of small effects required exceptional skill, patience and self-criticism."

Through Professor Arthur Schuster, who had resigned as Langworthy Professor of Physics in the University of Manchester, Rutherford was invited to accept the chair. He moved in 1907 to laboratories which were relatively well equipped for that time; the efficient organization of the Department of Physics left him much time for research rather than teaching and administration; and he was fortunate in finding an exceptionally capable lecture assistant and laboratory steward in Mr. W. Kay. Very

9

rapidly Rutherford developed a thriving school of research into radioactivity, his great energy and enthusiasm bringing many physicists from all over the world to work under his guidance. In their Obituary Notice for the Royal Society[5], Eve and Chadwick said:

"Two circumstances facilitated the beginning of work in Manchester. He found there Schuster's young assistant, H. Geiger, who became an admirable second in furthering the development of a research school; and in 1908 the Akademie der Wissenschaften of Vienna lent him 150 mgm of radium, a very considerable amount of radium in those days. The radium preparation was of low concentration and so bulky that it was unsuitable for most experiments. Rutherford therefore developed a new way of using radium – the use of radium in solution as a source for its emanation, which could be pumped off when required. The apparatus for this purpose and the methods of purifying the emanation were worked out with the aid of Royds (Phil. Mag., November, 1908). This was a significant advance in technique, for it made possible a regular supply of radium emanation and active deposit for the many experiments in progress in the laboratory.

Rutherford's work at McGill had firmly established the transformation theory propounded by himself and Soddy, and the general scheme of the radioactive families was sufficiently clear, at least in outline, by 1907. At the time of his arrival in Manchester he was more keenly interested in the radiations from the radioactive substances, and especially in the α-rays, than in the substances themselves.

One of the earliest major contributions in Manchester was the beautiful work with Geiger (Proc. Roy. Soc., vol. A 81, p. 141, 1908) in which the number of α-particles emitted per second per gramme of radium was accurately and directly measured for the first time. It is difficult now to realize the many difficulties which had to be overcome before they were able to detect a single α-particle by means of its electrical effect. It was a technical feat of a high order, all the more impressive for having been accomplished with the simplest apparatus and in a very short time. The result of this measurement was of the utmost value in general atomic theory, as well as in radioactivity. When combined with the measurement of the total charge carried by a stream of α-particles (Rutherford and Geiger, Proc. Roy. Soc., vol. A 81, p. 162, 1908) this result showed clearly that the normal α-particle was doubly charged, and gave a value for the unit of charge which was at least as reliable as any available at the time.

Rutherford's earlier work had convinced him (and most other physicists) that the α-particles were doubly-charged helium atoms. Although the new work with Geiger strongly supported this view, he evidently felt the need of a direct identification. This followed in the experiment with Royds (Phil. Mag., vol. 17, p. 281, 1909). [The glassblower, Baumbach,] succeeded in preparing glass tubes with walls so thin that α-particles could pass through and yet so strong as to withstand atmospheric pressure. Such an 'α-ray tube' was filled with radon and the emitted α-particles were allowed to emerge into a previously evacuated space. After a few days, an electrical discharge was passed through this space and the characteristic spectrum of helium appeared. This experiment created great interest on account of its simple directness and beauty.

A quantitative continuation of this work – the measurement of the rate of production of helium by radium – was carried out with his friend, B. B. Boltwood, who spent

11

a year's leave in Manchester (Phil. Mag., vol. 22, p. 586, 1911). This formed a fitting conclusion to this particular chapter of Rutherford's work on the α-particles, for, by combining these results with those of the counting experiments, it was possible to deduce Avogadro's number in the most direct manner conceivable. It is worth stressing that in principle Rutherford counted the number of molecules in a cubic centimetre of gas just as directly as one can count the number of marbles in a box. It is not a little remarkable that Rutherford, who, with Soddy, destroyed one of the most cherished beliefs of the atomists – that of the indestructibility of the atom – should also have been the one to provide some of the most convincing evidence of the existence of atoms, and to verify so brilliantly some of the predictions of the kinetic theory of gases."

Rutherford's great reputation however, was established by the extraordinary results of his work on the scattering of alpha-particles, work which was to bring about a complete revolution in knowledge of the structure of matter. In a series of papers[6], Geiger and Marsden showed that occasionally an alpha-particle appeared to be scattered backwards from matter, in a direction opposite to its initial path. Rutherford had realized previously that the alpha-particle was a helium atom, carrying two elementary charges of electricity, and moving with velocity of the order of that of light. He asked himself how such a swift particle could experience the enormous force required to turn it back upon its path. Assuming that this force is electrical in origin, that is that the alpha-particle is deflected by the Coulomb force, varying inversely as the square of the distance separating the alpha-particle from a scattering centre carrying charge Ze, Rutherford showed that in the case of gold, where Z was assumed to be about 100, the alpha-particle must penetrate to within a distance of about 3×10^{-12} cm of the scattering centre. The scattering centre must therefore be at least 10,000 times smaller in diameter than the atom in order to account for the scattering. On this assumption of a central, charged nucleus, Rutherford was able to calculate what should be the distribution in angle of alpha-particles scattered from a massive centre. Accurate observations by Geiger and Marsden showed that this calculated angular distribution was that observed, within the errors of experiment. Further experiments verified Rutherford's assumptions in every particular. The nuclear picture of the atom was firmly established.

A young theoretical physicist from Copenhagen, Niels Bohr, spent some months with Rutherford in Manchester after the middle of 1912, and began to think about the problem why the electron cloud, of diameter of the order of 10^{-8} cm, was not rapidly captured by the nucleus towards which it was attracted. Invoking the concept of the quantum of action put forward by Planck, he was able to produce a beautiful and convincing model of a stable nuclear atom, which, in the case of atomic hydrogen, accounted quantitatively for its optical spectrum. The Rutherford-Bohr model of the atom was subsequently refined and shown to account for all the general properties of matter. The reality of this model was demonstrated further by the brilliant work of Moseley in Rutherford's laboratory. Moseley established the relationship between the nuclear charge of an atom and the frequencies of the characteristic X-rays which it emitted, and was able to equate the atomic number of an element in the periodic table with the quantity Z of the nuclear charge, Ze.

Much work was done in Manchester upon the properties and nature of the beta and gamma-radiations from radio-active substances, work which was aided greatly by the

13

existence of a Readership in Mathematical Physics established by Schuster. It was held in turn by Bateman, Darwin and Bohr. In addition, important insight into the processes associated with the passage of charged particles through matter, and on the theory of X-ray reflection by crystals was developed by the theoreticians.

The total contribution made to physics in Rutherford's laboratory during this Manchester period was enormous, and most of it was due to Rutherford himself or to his inspiration of others. The work was terminated abruptly by the outbreak of the 1914–1918 War, the research workers mostly joining one of the fighting services. Rutherford became a member of the Panel of the Admiralty Board of Invention and Research, and worked on many problems, notably the detection and location of submarines. He undertook this work with his usual energy, in his laboratory, and at a research station at Aberdour, directed by Professor W. H. Bragg. He made a visit to the United States as a member of an Anglo-French mission to pool work on anti-submarine warfare. Though heavily engaged in this way he continued his university work, and even found time to carry further his academic researches. I quote again from the memoir by Eve and Chadwick*:

"Much of Rutherford's time was taken up by war work, as well as by the difficulties of running his department with a heavily depleted staff. In 1919, however, he was able to publish the result of yet another epoch-making research, again made with α-particles. In four papers published in the Philosophical Magazine, vol. 37, he proved conclusively that the long range particles earlier shown by Marsden to be produced when α-particles were fired into hydrogen were in fact fast hydrogen nuclei, and he showed that identical particles were

* A. S. Eve and J. Chadwick, loc. cit.

14

produced by the collisions of α-particles with nitrogen. The explanation – that these protons were the result of the disruption, or 'artificial disintegration', of the normally stable nitrogen nucleus – was so revolutionary, and so pregnant with far-reaching implications, that it clearly needed to be supported by very complete experimental evidence. Rutherford obtained the necessary support by an admirably designed series of control experiments. He did the whole of the experimental work, with Kay's assistance in taking observations of scintillations. The further development of this work, and its extension to other nuclei, belongs to the Cambridge period."

In 1919, through the enthusiastic advocacy of Joseph Larmor, Rutherford received an invitation to fill the Cavendish Chair of Physics in Cambridge, in succession to his teacher, Sir J. J. Thomson, who had been elected Master of Trinity College. It was only after considerable heart-searching and hesitation that he accepted. He wrote to Thomson saying that no advantages of the Cavendish

".... could possibly compensate for any disturbance of our long friendship or for any possible friction, whether open or latent, that might possibly arise if we did not have a clear mutual understanding with regard to the laboratory and Research Students. ...."

The reply was reassuring, welcoming the possibility that Rutherford was interested and giving a definite undertaking that if he went he would have an absolutely free hand in the management of the Laboratory. Some doubts remained, for on 15th March, 1919, he wrote to Sir Arthur Schuster, whom he had succeeded in Manchester, and with whom he had formed a lasting friendship:

"Dear Schuster,

Larmor, I believe, told you they are wanting me to be a candidate for the Cavendish Chair and I expect you know the arrangements whereby J.J.T. has to have his own rooms, mechanic, etc., and to have research people to work with him. Of course the post has many attractions but has some obvious disadvantages and difficulties. As the time approaches for a definite decision, I find myself oscillating a good deal between the relative certainties of Manchester (including a fine Lab and a show of my own) and the advantages of Cambridge as a place to live in and opportunities for advancing Physics. At the same time, the presence of J.J.T., working in a part of the Lab even without technical power has certain obvious difficulties which are not diminished by the fact that our lines of work are very parallel. Well I expect you can envisage the situation from the point of view of an outsider and as you were responsible for transplanting me to Manchester and for complete effacement of yourself from the Lab there, I would like your frank opinions of whether you think I should go or stay. I may mention that the War has of course played havoc with the staff and research of the Lab here and a fresh start has to be made here in any case. At the same time, the family are a little tired of life in this grimy city and in this respect Cambridge has a distinct pull. Well, if you feel like expressing an opinion, please do so soon as I shall have to make the irreversible decision by the end of the week. Larmor is doing everything in his power to make the post as comfortable as possible and is very pressing as also are other Cambridge people.

E.R."

This was followed by a further letter indicating that the balance tended to move towards continuing in Manchester:

16

Mch 23. 1919.

"Dear Schuster,

I find after sending you my letter that you are an elector for the Cavendish Chair. Please excuse the indiscretion of writing to one officially immersed in the question.

It has been a worrying problem what to do but I think Manchester has first call under the conditions.

Yours sincerely,
E. Rutherford"

Rutherford accepted the Cavendish Chair when Sir Joseph Larmor and the electoral committee agreed that he should be both Cavendish Professor and Director of the Cavendish Laboratory.

REFERENCES

1. H. Tizard, Journal of the Chemical Society of London, p. 980 (October, 1946).
2 A.S. Eve, "Rutherford": Cambridge, 1939.
3 Otto Hahn, Nature, vol. 140, p. 1052 (1937).
4 J.J. Thomson, Nature, vol. 140, p. 752 (1937).
5 A.S. Eve and J. Chadwick, Obituary Notices of Fellows of the Royal Society, No. 6, vol. 2, pp. 394–423 (1938).
6 Geiger and Marsden, Proc. Roy. Soc., vol. 82, p. 495 (1909); Rutherford, Phil. Mag., vol. 21, p. 660 (1911).

CHAPTER 1

The Cavendish Laboratory

In September, 1925, the Rutherfords visited Adelaide, where I was working as assistant to the Professor of Physics, Kerr Grant. Rutherford gave a talk in the Department of Physics on the work going on in the Cavendish Laboratory. This fascinated me, and I determined that I would work under him, if this were at all possible. At that time, members of the University as humble as I were not introduced to such illustrious visitors. In 1927 I was able to convince the Commissioners for the Exhibition of 1851 that I should be awarded an overseas scholarship. Professor Kerr Grant was abroad on sabbatical leave, and had just visited the Cavendish. He wrote a letter urging me to endeavour to go to Cambridge, where he had found a more lively atmosphere than in any other physical laboratory in England. I had already telegraphed to Rutherford and had received a reply saying that he would reserve a place for me. I had also been accepted by Trinity College as a Research Student. So I set out convinced that I had made the right decision.

THE NEWCOMER

I arrived in the Cavendish in October, 1927, as a raw research student from the antipodes, whom Rutherford had kindly admitted to what was then, by far, the greatest physical laboratory in the world. I was told to wait outside his office by a formidable little man, Mr. Hayles, who while primarily the lecture assistant, acted as his secretary. In the passage, with uncarpeted board floor, dingy varnished pine doors and stained plastered walls, indifferently lit by a skylight with dirty glass, I found myself in the company of another Australian, Cecil Eddy, and a young physicist from Trinity College, Dublin, E. T. S. Walton. Each of us expressed agreement at the unprepossessing appearance of the Laboratory tucked away obscurely in the narrow Free School Lane, behind Corpus Christi College, and we speculated about the Cavendish Professor who would interview us shortly. When my turn came, I entered a small office littered with books and papers, the desk cluttered in a manner which I had been taught at school indicated an untidy and inefficient mind. It was raining, and drops of water ran reluctantly down the grime covered glass of the uncurtained window.

I was received genially by a large, rather florid man, with thinning fair hair and a large moustache, who reminded me forcibly of the keeper of the general store and post office in a little village in the hills behind Adelaide where I had spent part of my childhood. Rutherford made me feel welcome and at ease at once. He spluttered a little as he talked, from time to time holding a match to a pipe which produced smoke and ash like a volcano. Later on, I found that he reduced his tobacco to tinder dryness on a newspaper spread out before the fire at his home, or on a radiator in the laboratory, before putting it in his pouch. He was most interested to know that I was accompanied by a young wife, and immediately asked us to tea at Newnham Cottage on the following Sunday. I told him of my wish to do some work on the effects on metals of bombardment by positive ions, if he thought that would fit well into the program of the laboratory, and handed him a paper which

19

I had written on the adsorption of gases on a freshly formed surface of pure mercury. He went over my proposals for my work and agreed that I should do as I wished, saying that he would read the paper and advise me whether it should be published, and where. He then told me to go round the Laboratory and make myself known to:

"... the boys, particularly Aston and J.J., whom you will find working in the Garage or in nearby rooms, and who should be interested in what you want to do."

As I hesitated at the door, intending to ask where this 'Garage' was located, he boomed cheerfully:

"Now don't be diffident. Tell them all I sent you."

As I left, two large young men strode from a room opposite, nearly colliding with the very diffident newcomer. With a charming smile, a handsome and impressive man said:

"I'm Blackett. This is Dymond. Who are you?"

These members of the Laboratory were clearly friendly. I told them of my instructions and my lack of knowledge of the geography of the Laboratory. They led me down the stairs to the open door of the large basement laboratory known as the Garage, and told me that I would find J.J.'s set-up in the far corner, and Aston in a room beyond. Reluctantly, I made my way towards the place where two men worked whom I regarded with the same awe as I did Rutherford, and whom I had never thought to meet in the flesh. Fortunately for me, neither J.J. nor Aston was in, so I was saved considerable embarrassment, but J.J.'s assistants, Everett and Morley, chatted with me for a while mostly about the pleasures of motor cycling. They were in attendance upon an amazing mass of glass tubing, taps and flasks, spread over two or three tables, and covered with dust. I had the impression that it had grown continuously since J.J. discovered the electron thirty years previously, each new experiment being added, and nothing ever removed or cleaned.

This was my introduction to Rutherford and the Cavendish Laboratory. Rutherford's warm welcome and interest, combined with my conviction that I could do better glass-blowing myself than J.J.'s assistants were able to accomplish, gave me courage. I went to see my tutor in Trinity College with greater self-assurance. The Cavendish and Cambridge were already becoming part of me.

Trinity was Rutherford's College. There he had been the first research student, and when he became Cavendish Professor of Physics it was natural that the College should elect him to a Professorial Fellowship. He had a great affection for Trinity, and especially for the company at High Table on Sunday evenings. Unfortunately for me, the tutor to whom I was assigned was an American and a non-scientist, who had become more English than the English. He took little interest in a research student in physics, while the College was so large that it was not easy for a man from the Dominions, who had not obtained his first degree in Cambridge, to adapt himself readily to its archaic practices. Hence, I got less from Trinity than I should have, largely through my own fault.

SUNDAY TEA AND OTHER MATTERS

On Sunday afternoons during term the Rutherfords entertained members of the Cavendish Laboratory and their wives to tea at 4.30 p.m., a good mixture of seniors and juniors being present on each occasion. There was a certain formality about the issuing of invitations, and those present were expected by Lady Rutherford to write notes of thanks afterwards, in the accepted manner of the time. We were met at the door by a maid in cap and apron, and ushered into the fine living room, where we were greeted by our hosts and seated in chairs placed in the arc of a circle.

Lady Rutherford poured the tea, while Rutherford himself kept up a lively conversation. As research students, we regarded these occasions much as our elders would a summons to Buckingham Palace, wearing our best suits and dresses and arriving punctiliously on the stroke of half past four. (On one early occasion, we were greatly embarrassed to find that we had arrived an hour late, having failed to reset our watches for the change to summer time!) However, once seated there was no differentiation between junior and senior, the Rutherfords drawing everyone into discussion of whatever topic was introduced. An hour or a little more later, if it was fine outside, we were asked by Lady Rutherford whether we would like to see the garden, and after a stroll round we were led firmly to the door in the outer wall, where we shook hands and departed. If the weather was bad or the light had gone, the end of the occasion was signalled by Lady Rutherford rising and going round the circle bidding us good-bye. There was no opportunity to outstay our welcome.

Rutherford's handshake was in marked contrast with his welcoming voice and manner. His "Hello my boy!" was accompanied by a very brief, limp and boneless clasp of the hand, and rarely by a slap on the back or a hand on the shoulder. He gave the impression that he was shy of physical contact with another person.

A written invitation to tea on our first Sunday came from Lady Rutherford. We duly arrived at Newnham Cottage promptly at 4.30 p.m., to find there a group of about ten people, to whom we were introduced. Lady Rutherford was short and plump, with a rather abrupt manner, a little forbidding at first. She addressed every man as "Mister", whether he was a new research student, or the very senior Dr. F. W. Aston. Among the guests were Dr. Peter Kapitza and his relatively new wife, Anna. Rutherford told with gusto and obvious affection how the Kapitzas had met in

Paris and had been married there. His warming interest in his younger colleagues is evident in a letter to Kapitza dated 29th April, 1927:

"My dear Kapitza,

I received your letter at breakfast this morning, and I read it with much interest and amusement. I wish you and your wife all happiness in your new state. I told Chadwick this morning and I think he is communicating with you.

You ask me to get a visa for Mrs. Kapitza but your state of mind is shown by the fact that you did not mention any of the necessary details, maiden name, age, etc., for that document. If the young lady has already been in England she must have a visa of her own which should be available for the purpose of her re-admission, unless her marriage invalidates it. In any case, send me all the necessary details. I will expect to see you back in the Laboratory before long. I will, of course, attend to the payment of cheques etc.

My wife and I unite in sending our warmest congratulations on the event and our best wishes for the future. They say it is a bad wife that does not help a little, so I shall expect your work to make even faster progress.

Yours very sincerely,
E. Rutherford

I am not surprised at the news as I had heard rumours of your magnetic susceptibility under intense alternating fields!
E. R."

The gentle hint that the honeymoon should not be too

prolonged was characteristic of his interest in Kapitza's career as a scientist, as well as in his personal happiness.

During my early years in the Cavendish, I attended several courses of lectures. Aston's lectures on isotopes and mass-spectroscopy were dull because he read them directly from his book on the subject. Eddington discussed relativity almost without mathematics. I enjoyed his lectures because of the speculative interludes, but cannot say that I learnt much relativity from them. Hartree, on quantum theory, was pedantic but thorough and helpful, and Mott's later series on the same subject was excellent. C. T. R. Wilson's lectures on atmospheric electricity began with a crowded classroom, but the audience for the third lecture was four, including one man who was doing research with C.T.R., and could not easily drop out, and a kindly American college professor, who felt that it would be too pointed to cease attending when the audience was three. I did not attend after the third, not because the subject lacked interest, but because the lecturer himself was so clearly embarrassed by his inability to express himself. His were the most painful lectures I ever experienced. In contrast, the very youthful Jack Ratcliffe's talks on the ionosphere were the most lucid and best presented lectures I have attended.

Each year, Rutherford gave a course of lectures on general atomic physics. He had to go to London often for meetings, and it then fell to my lot, for two years, to give some of these lectures for him. On these occasions, he would call me into his office to sit beside him while he explained what I should talk about, with the aid of an extraordinary collection of notes, written on odd scraps of paper and

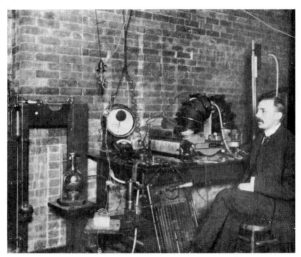

Borrowed cuffs – McGill, 1905

The Cavendish Laboratory. Old Entrance in
Free School Lane

Rutherford, circa 1932

Newnham Cottage. Walnut tree in foreground

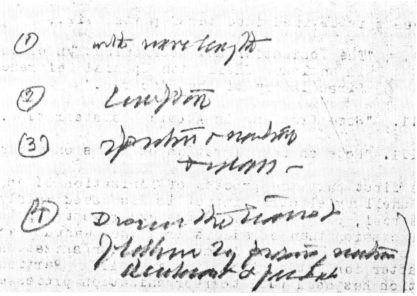

Example of Rutherford's handwriting. Notes for lecture to students (pencil)

EXAMPLES OF RUTHERFORD'S HANDWRITING

End of letter to M.L.O., 1931 (ink)

Notes for lecture in Göttingen (ink)

pinned together in the right order. He had used these notes for many years, so that there were copious amendments and additions, always in pencil, some of which had become almost too faint to read. We went through these carefully, sometimes for an hour or more, adding, crossing out, and getting the papers into a hopeless disorder. It was necessary for me set to work to construct my own notes, following his as closely as I could, though this was not always possible. Since the request to deputize for him came only 24 hours or less before the lecture, this was quite a task. However, I found going through the lecture with him an experience of great interest, for I saw what he regarded as important and what could well be omitted, decisions not in accord with most textbooks. When I argued a point, or asked for clarification, his physical insight into the behaviour of atoms and their nuclei became apparent. It was at these times that I grew to appreciate his profound sense of history. He understood how knowledge grew and how spasmodically new ideas were born.

In Rutherford's discussion of magnetic phenomena, as part of these lectures, he derived the expression for the work done in a hysteresis cycle:

$$W = \int H\,dH + \int H\,dB, \qquad \text{round the cycle.}$$

There was a story told that on one occasion he knew that he had to get rid of the first term in the expression, but had forgotten just how:

"Integral $H\,dH$ vanishes, eh, eh; integral $H\,dH$ vanishes, eh, eh." And then triumphantly: "Integral $H\,dH$ vanishes because $d\,H$ is so small!"

If this is not a true story, it ought to be, for it is characteristic of his approach – when he knew the answer he did not care by what route he arrived. I remember his derivation of the classical radius of the electron. Having become tangled in the algebra on the black-board, he turned to the class saying:

"You can derive that for yourselves. It is very simple, and in any case, has very little meaning!"

Soon afterwards, in dealing with early experiments on the apparent increase of mass of the electron with its kinetic energy, reaching a similar impasse, he turned irritably to the class:

"You sit there like a lot of numbskulls, and not one of you can tell me where I've gone wrong."

Rutherford regarded the mathematics as a mode of expression of the physics, and for him there was no other reason for its existence. He was not a good lecturer, in the ordinary sense of the word, except when dealing with some recent ideas of his own. He hummed and hahed too much, repeating himself when he lost his place, but he was so enthusiastic, so imbued with the excitement of physics, that he was inspiring. He was convinced that nature was inherently simple, and that apparent complexity reflected lack of knowledge:

"I believe these things to be simple, being a simple man myself."

Dr. Bretscher has recalled this incident:

"One morning at 10 or 11.0 a.m., I went to the Prof's office as he had asked me to see him. I knocked timidly, heard some noise which encouraged me to open the door and proceeded to enter his office. I was, however, confronted by a furious Lordship shouting at me that he was very busy and could not see me.

Rather shocked I rushed out of his office to cogitate what particular crime I had unknowingly committed, but I could not think of anything I had done which could possibly deserve such reaction from the great man. So I went to see Dr. Oliphant who could perhaps tell me how I could avoid in future such an explosion. On

26

hearing the story Oliphant broke into uncontrollable laughter explaining to me that the Prof. could not find his lecture notes and had in a few minutes to face an expectant audience of students. As it turned out I rather enjoyed the experience in retrospect."

ARITHMETIC

Rutherford had great ability at arithmetic which he did rapidly and with uncanny accuracy, despite the apparently crude approximations which he used. Wherever possible, he reduced multiplication to addition and subtraction, mumbling to himself as he did a calculation. Thus, to convert the mass change which occurred in a nuclear reaction from atomic mass units to MeV, he would multiply by 1,000 and subtract 7 per cent, while to square Avogadro's number, 6.0248×10^{23}, he would multiply 6 by 6.05, obtaining for the digital part, 36.30, as against the actual value, 36.298. Moreover, he would remember that at one stage he had over-estimated a little and would under-estimate later. His results were always within the limits of error of an experiment, or of the accuracy of the constants used. Dr. A. E. Kempton recalls that, at 22 years of age, he thought himself rather good at arithmetic, both in speed and accuracy, but that he found Rutherford, at that time 65 years old, to be at least his equal.

Rutherford appeared to possess no fountain pen. He signed letters and documents with an old fashioned steel-nib pen, writing slowly and awkwardly. He carried, in a bottom waistcoat pocket, three or four stumps of pencils, never more than two inches in length and with very short and blunt points. When necessary he fumbled for one of these, which he held in a cramped manner between thumb and forefinger. With this also, he never wrote rapidly, but with deliberation. Sometimes the pencil was so blunt that the words were all but indecipherable, though generally his meaning was clear.

THEORETICIANS

Rutherford's daughter and only child, Eileen, had married Professor Ralph Fowler, Smith's Prizeman and author of a comprehensive treatise on statistical mechanics. It was through his efforts, and his influence on young mathematicians, that a school of theoretical physics grew up in Cambridge. Though not himself in the front rank of those who were fertile in theoretical physics, Fowler had immense mathematical ability which he placed freely and generously at the disposal of the experimenters. I owe him much for his patient attention to my trivial difficulties. He gathered round him a kaleidoscopic group of gifted theoreticians, especially those fleeing from Hitler's Germany. Many, if not most, of the older theoreticians of distinction throughout the western world today, spent some time in Cambridge with Fowler. Despite, perhaps because of, this close personal relationship with theoreticians, and his great affection for Niels Bohr, Rutherford never ceased to tease "our theoretical friends", as he called them. At question time, following lectures at which he had presided, he would probe mercilessly after the physics behind their mathematical techniques, often declaring:

"I am a simple man and I want a simple answer."

I once heard him say to Heisenberg, in proposing a vote of thanks for his lectures:

"We are all much obliged for your exposition of a lot of interesting nonsense, which is most suggestive."

After the Scott Lectures on the uncertainty principle, by Niels Bohr, he remarked: "You know Bohr, your conclusions seem to me to be as uncertain as the premises upon which they are built."

But this raillery, and his distrust of complex theory which could not be expressed in visual terms, concealed a deep respect and affection for those who contributed, in the theoretical field, to the advance of physics.

Rutherford was not interested much in exact measurement of physical quantities for its own sake. He contended that this was the job of National Physical Laboratories and Standards Laboratories, rather than of the Cavendish. When an experiment had yielded sufficient information to enable a reasonable interpretation of the results, he encouraged his colleagues to move on to something else:

"There is always someone, somewhere, without ideas of his own, who will measure that accurately. Have you thought of trying so and so?"

He was impatient of too much time spent in the interests of accuracy, or reliable performance, in the construction of apparatus. When I was setting up a semi-circular magnetic focussing system for the separation of the isotopes of potassium, in an attempt to determine which of the isotopes was radioactive, he remarked irritably after some weeks of abortive effort:

"For God's sake use wide slits. You can always narrow them down later and, in any case, a very partial separation will give the answer."

To a research student from New Zealand, busily at work on a lathe making part of what he hoped would be a superior expansion chamber, he said jovially, but with considerable implied meaning:

"Well, Y, still making and breaking? When are you going to do some physics?"

29

However, when it was necessary, in the interests of physical interpretation, to know some quantity with accuracy, he did not hesitate to encourage precision. Because at least one alpha-particle energy should be known accurately, as a reference value for other particle energies, he readily provided facilities for George Briggs to measure the energy of the alpha-particles from polonium as well as he could, by magnetic deflection. After Rosenblum, in Paris, had shown that complex alpha-particle groups could be better resolved by focussing in the large electromagnet built by Cotton than by the differential range technique used in the Cavendish, Rutherford got Cockcroft to design a magnet like a double mushroom, which was simple and far less expensive than Cotton's magnet, and gave Wynn-Williams and others the task of measuring accurately the energy differences between the alpha-particle groups from all the products of radium and thorium which emitted these particles. The reason for this was his desire to correlate the energies of the gamma-rays and beta-rays, as measured by C. D. Ellis in the Cavendish, with the differences in the energies of the various alpha-particle groups. Dr. W. B. Lewis has written to me recalling an occasion when Rutherford, explaining to a visitor what the magnet was used for, said:

"Yes, it cost £250, a lot of money, as much as a research student for a year, but it will do a lot more work!"

ORDERS OF MAGNITUDE

Rutherford believed that if a research worker had an idea of the order of magnitude of the quantities he had to deal with, he was unlikely to make serious errors in his calculations. For this reason he was fond of asking seemingly elementary questions in oral examinations for the Ph.D. Degree. For instance.

"What is the resistance of a piece of wire?"

"What sort of wire, of what diameter and length?"

"Any old piece of wire".

The candidate who answered 1,000 ohms or one thousandth of an ohm was asked to justify his statement. He who said a fraction of an ohm, say one tenth or one hundredth, was judged to have the right idea. Another question was:

"What is the inductance of a wedding ring?"

He expected the answer:

"Of the order of its diameter, say one centimetre."

He would then go on to ask what would happen if a bar magnet, on the axis of the ring but some centimetres away, was suddenly pushed towards the ring? This would be followed up with a query, what difference would it make if the ring were superconducting? In these ways, besides his searching out of a young man's sense of magnitudes, Rutherford would obtain much information about his knowledge of some fundamental physical phenomena.

Rutherford was very conscious of the nervousness of a candidate appearing before such august examiners. He would guide his answers till he settled down. On an occasion when a young man, all too conscious of the limits of his knowledge, was asked by Rutherford's co-examiner about a complex feature of the theory of band-spectra and was fumbling badly, Rutherford suddenly said:

"X, you've asked a question about which I know nothing. The candidate is obviously in the same position and I can't say that I blame him. What about your going to the board and telling us both about it?"

The co-examiner had then to admit that he could not do so. He remembered vaguely reading something about it, and thought it would be a good question.

Each year, the members of the Cavendish Laboratory entertained the Professor at dinner. A distinguished guest proposed the toast of the Laboratory and the Professor replied. On one occasion, following a very polished speech by Sir William Bragg in which he described the dovetailing histories of the much older Royal Institution, in London, and the Cavendish, Rutherford was moved to recall, for our benefit, conditions when he was a research student in New Zealand. He described how his first task each morning was to assemble his battery of Grove cells, consisting of plates of zinc and platinum immersed in dilute sulphuric and fuming nitric acids respectively, the liquids separated by a porous cell. The only voltmeter in the laboratory was of the hot wire type, in which a current caused a long platinum wire to expand and rotate a pointer. It was necessary to take a reading rather rapidly, as its resistance was so low that it rapidly ran down the battery if left connected. At the end of the day, the battery had to be dismantled, the acids returned to storage bottles, and the electrodes and porous cells thoroughly washed out. In the Cavendish, a small Hampshire liquid air machine had recently been installed, when he arrived. This was very erratic in performance and required constant nursing by the technicians. Rutherford spoke feelingly of research workers waiting impatiently to collect their share of the trickle of liquid which the machine sometimes produced.

On another such occasion, when C. T. R. Wilson, having won the Nobel Prize, was guest of honour, Rutherford told us of going to Wilson's room to say goodbye before leaving to take up his appointment at McGill University, in Montreal. C. T. R. was sitting at a bench littered with the remnants of his efforts at glass-blowing. As they talked, he continued to grind the rounded end of a piece of glass tubing held in one hand, into a shoulder in a second piece of glass tubing held in the other. He was making a valve for one of his early expansion chambers. When they had shaken hands and Rutherford was about to leave, he resumed his grinding operation. Some years passed before Rutherford visited England again and called on C.T.R. in the Cavendish. He swore that he found him sitting at the same bench, grinding the same pieces of his glass valve together! Rutherford's story was illustrated with hand motions imitating those of C.T.R., while Wilson himself, the guest of honour at Rutherford's side, listened attentively with a faint smile. He did not deny the truth of the tale.

HUMAN RELATIONS

Despite Rutherford's expectation of high performance from his research students and colleagues, he retained a fatherly interest in all who had worked with him. A considerable part of his correspondence was with students who had not distinguished themselves in any way, often for reasons which he realized made effective research very difficult or impossible.

Rutherford enjoyed the company of his fellows, whatever their interests, colour, creed, or social standing. There was no trace of condescension in his manner when talking about the furnaces and boilers in a ship's engine room with stokers or greasers. His attitude towards all at the captain's table was precisely the same. He never forgot to thank personally the technicians who had assisted with a lecture which he had given. As chairman of a meeting he was polite and considerate of all, however fatuous some contributions may have been, and he showed special sympathy towards the young and inexperienced. He realized the particular difficulties of those who came from abroad – difficulties of

33

language, of a background of physics which was not a good preparation for research, or of coming to terms with a strange environment. He helped students who found themselves in financial difficulties, though sometimes repayment was long dealyed. Lady Rutherford told me that he could never resist a personal appeal for funds in support of any charity, and that often she had to step in and prevent him from giving away far more than they could afford. His charity was always private.

Rutherford's goodwill extended to all mankind. He often discussed with me how the extreme poor of India or Africa could be helped, declaring that only science and technology could offer solutions to this difficult problem. At a time when the question of over-population, and the ills which followed from it, were scarcely talked about or realized, he spoke of the necessity for birth control to limit the demand on the world's resources. However, he continued to believe that there was good in the colonial system, and much that the richer nations could contribute towards the betterment of colonial peoples before they could govern themselves.

Rutherford was completely happy in his work. He believed that most men could share his contentment if they sought out and pursued goals which they set for themselves. He did not believe that anyone, other than a person himself, could make the choice of work in which satisfaction could be found, and thought that better methods to fit men to jobs should be developed and used. In this, he was at one with Bertrand Russell, who said that the world would be an infinitely pleasanter place if men would but learn to seek their own happiness, rather than the misery of others.

CHAPTER 2

Counting, Money and Mass Spectroscopy

COUNTING

When I arrived in Cambridge, Rutherford and Chadwick were still working together on the disintegration of light nuclei by bombardment with alpha-particles. They used a zinc sulphide scintillation screen and microscope of high light gathering power to detect the product protons, working with dark-adapted eyes in an underground laboratory in the older part of the Cavendish. They were helped by Rutherford's research assistant, George Crowe, who had prepared most of the radioactive sources under Chadwick's watchful eye.

Scintillation counting, especially for the detection of protons as the rare product of a nuclear transformation, was a slow and tiring task, requiring great concentration by the observer. Chadwick has written to me: "The normal procedure was for an observer to count for one minute (sometimes less), being then relieved by another observer, and each observer might have up to 20 periods of one minute each during an experiment. The total duration of an experiment was limited by the decay of the active deposit source, as well as by the fatigue of the observers."

Chadwick has told[1] that it was when waiting between bouts of counting, or for eyes to become dark-adapted, that Rutherford would speak far more frankly of his speculations about nuclear properties and structure, and of other matters, than he did in daylight.

35

Techniques for counting alpha-particles and protons in the Cavendish Laboratory were revolutionized by a very ingenious Welshman, Wynn-Williams, who has not received the recognition which I believe to be his due. Following the work of Greinacher in Vienna, he and Ward developed in the Cavendish linear amplifiers which would respond quantitatively to the very small current pulse produced in a shallow ionization chamber by the passage of a single fast particle. Such a chamber produced a pulse, easily distinguishable from the background of noise, from 1 or 2 mm of an alpha-particle track. The much lower ionizing power of electrons meant that beta and gamma-radiation added to the noise without obscuring the alpha-particle pulses if their intensity was not too great. The amplitude of the pulse was proportional to the ionizing power of the particle, so that, with proper precautions, protons could be readily distinguished from alpha-particles. The new electronic systems of Wynn-Williams replaced the tedious scintillation techniques, could count at rates thousands of times greater, produced no fatigue in the operator, and could give permanent visual records on photographic film or paper with the aid of an oscillograph. Rutherford realized that by making the particle traverse two identical ionization chambers in series, and collecting both ionization currents on the same intermediate thin metal foil electrode, only particles which ended their range in one chamber or the other would produce pulses. In this way, it was possible to detect relatively low intensity groups of particles of smaller energy, in a large flux of more energetic particles. Wynn-Williams and Ward were joined by W. B. Lewis in the further development of this powerful technique, and of fast discriminatory digital counting circuitry, using thyratrons initially, which replaced photographic recording and measurement of amplitudes of pulses. They revolutionized the rate at which statistically significant results in nuclear physics were obtained in the laboratory. As already mentioned, they themselves, with Rutherford, applied these methods to the accurate analysis of alpha-particle groups using the mushroom magnet. But they generously built and supplied amplifiers, ionization chambers and counting circuits, for the use of all who needed them.

Shallow counting chambers with windows of thin foil, and the high-gain amplifiers used at that time, were sensitive to noise and vibration. While counting, one moved about on tiptoe and avoided knocking the benches or speaking loudly. Rutherford seldom remembered this, and when going the rounds of the Laboratory would thump in, hang his umbrella over the back of a chair from which it clattered onto the floor, and would begin a conversation in a voice which he was incapable of making a whisper. With a sigh, one watched the oscillograph spot careering, wildly over the screen, and cancelled that particular count, or part of a count.

At about this time, Geiger visited the Laboratory and told us of his development of a new variety of the Geiger-Müller counter, using a central wire electrode down the axis of a metal cylinder, in place of the point or ball electrodes used in the past. These counters worked at low pressures and at lower voltages, were much more sensitive, and with suitable electronic circuitry had a rapid recovery time, enabling much faster counting of beta and gamma-rays.

P.M.S. Blackett worked in a room close to the space allotted to me. He was a pioneer of the automatically recycling expansion chamber taking photographs on film continuously. He had inherited the equipment devised by Shimizu, who returned to Japan, and modified it considerably. He had already obtained stereoscopic pictures of the disintegration of the nitrogen nucleus when bombarded by alpha-particles, confirming the transformation first observed in Manchester by Rutherford and his colleagues some years earlier, using scintillation methods. He turned his attention to studies of cosmic radiation, with Geiger counters to initiate an expansion only when the chamber, situated in a magnetic field, had been traversed by an ionizing particle. For his work he was awarded the Nobel Prize in 1948, long after he had left the Cavendish. Blackett was a tall, handsome man, with a forceful personality, whose lectures were very good. He had a non-conformist mind in the conformist society of Cambridge. In later years, Blackett was critical of Rutherford for not seizing the opportunities arising from the great discoveries made in the Cavendish in the early 1930's. He felt that Rutherford could have exploited the unique situation to make the Laboratory continue as the world centre of nuclear and particle physics.

MONEY AND MODESTY

It is difficult to reconcile all that was accomplished in the Cavendish under Rutherford with the accounts of receipts and expenditures published in the University Reporter. Such figures can be incomplete and sometimes misleading, but they do convey the general picture. In 1921, the total expenditure by the University under the heading Experimental Physics, including salaries and wages, was £8,764, of which £7,710 came from fees paid by students. Apparatus and materials cost £2,548 and fuel, water, gas and electricity cost £328. By 1925 expenditure reached £9,628. In 1930 the Cavendish Laboratory cost £15,274, £230 above receipts for the year. (£812 was spent on equipment for Cockcroft and Walton's high potential laboratory, and on liquid air plant.) To this must be added £2,622 provided by the Department of Scientific and Industrial Research for the Magnetic Research Laboratory under Kapitza. In 1935 the University contributed £16,200 towards the expenses of the Laboratory, just over £1,000 being spent on apparatus and £30 on an international conference. Of course, there were additional sums not shown in these accounts, such as dividends from College Fellowships and for College supervision paid to members of staff and Research Fellows, research scholarships of various kinds held by graduate students and some small gifts of equipment, etc. However, research workers provided their own laboratory coats, notebooks, etc., and some of their own equipment. For instance, I paid £24 for a metal mercury diffusion pump in 1928 and unrecorded sums on tools, glass-blowing torch and rare gases, when my total income was £250 per annum. We typed our own papers and met the cost of reprints.

Rutherford disliked large and expensive equipment and resented the time-absorbing administrative problems associated with financing, planning and organization of a laboratory in which it was installed. He was quite depressed when, towards the end of his life, a large gift from Lord Austin enabled a new, modern building to be erected. He gladly handed over supervision of the planning to Cockcroft, to whom he had been delegating more and more of such tasks.

Chadwick has written to me about this aspect of Rutherford's character:

"One evening after dinner I was alone in the Combination Room (of Caius College) with the Master, Sir Hugh Anderson, when he suddenly said to me: 'Why wouldn't Rutherford accept the grant I had arranged for him?'

I could only reply that I knew nothing whatever about the matter; R. had not mentioned it to me. (He never did; nor to anyone, as far as I know).

39

The Master then told me the story. As I knew, Anderson had a great admiration for Rutherford. He thought that the grant made by the University to the Cavendish for research expenses was not sufficient to enable R. to pursue his work properly, but it was as much as the University could find and there was no possibility of increasing it. But Anderson's regard for R.'s work was such that he felt something must be done to help him. Accordingly, he approached a number of his wealthy friends and persuaded them to offer R. a private grant of £2,000 a year for some years to use at his discretion. He told R. what he had arranged. The position was that R. had only to say that he needed this money for researches in the Cavendish, and it would be forthcoming.

But R. did nothing, to Anderson's astonishment and indeed exasperation. I could offer no explanation for R.'s refusal to say that he needed more money for research. I knew so well how hampered and restricted R. was for lack of equipment and technical assistance, and his attitude was quite incomprehensible to me.

This conversation took place at some time between 1922 and 1925. It was only some years later that the explanation dawned on me.

It came about in this way.

One day I had taken R. up to the Radium Room so that he could assure himself that all was in order. We had at that time about 400 mgm. Ra in solution for the preparation of radon and active deposits sources. I remember well how, as we were coming down the stairs, I said that we did not have enough radium, so that I had to allocate sources very carefully to meet the demands; and I said what a pity it was that somebody or other had not made a gift to him of a gram of radium, as the women of the United States had made to Madame Curie. His reply astounded me. It was:

The 'Mushroom' Magnet

R.H. Fowler F.W. Aston   Rutherford   G.I. Taylor
South Africa, 1929, British Association meeting

Disturbing the counters!

'Well my boy, I am very glad nobody did. Just think: at the end of every year I should have to say what I had done with it. How on earth could I justify the use of a whole gram of radium?'

This was said quite seriously.

I had, of course, long realized that R. was modest about his achievements, notwithstanding his eager enjoyment of his reputation, his almost boyish delight in any laudatory references to his work, his susceptibility to flattery – aspects of his character with which you must be familiar. But I had not realized how deeply ingrained his modesty was until I pondered over this remark. And it threw a light on some arguments concerning the spending of money on research, especially on his own work. It was then that I thought that I had an explanation for his refusal to ask for the research subsidy which Sir Hugh Anderson had arranged for him; he did not feel that he could justify spending so much money – for it was a great deal in those days – on himself and his research students. And this in spite of his unique position in the scientific world, his extraordinary achievements in the past, and the urgent need to press on with the establishment of nuclear physics as a new branch of enquiry.

He was in truth, deeply modest."

Schonland recalled that Rutherford, irritated by a statement that research was not possible without adequate equipment remarked that he could do research at the North Pole!

In an article on Rutherford in "Sputnik" Magazine, Academician Kapitza writes:

"I remember a conversation I had with him during dinner at Trinity College. I do not remember how the conversation started – perhaps it was under the influence

41

of Lombroso's book, 'Genius and Madness.' I was expressing the view that every good scientist must to some extent be a madman. Rutherford overheard this conversation and asked me, 'In your opinion, Kapitza, am I mad too?' 'Yes Professor,' I replied. 'How are you going to prove it?' he asked. 'Very simply,' I replied. 'Perhaps you remember a few days ago you mentioned a letter you had received from the U.S.A., from a big American company. In this letter they offered to build you a colossal laboratory in America, and to pay you a fabulous salary. You only laughed at the offer, and would not consider it seriously. I think you will agree with me that from the point of view of a normal person you acted like a madman!' Rutherford laughed. He agreed that in all probability I was right."

I do not know whether Rutherford was the author of the words he often quoted: "Research in physics is ninety per cent perspiration, and only ten per cent inspiration", but he did believe in hard work and admired greatly those who got on with the job. He went round the Laboratory often, but at irregular intervals, and sat or stood chatting, pipe in hand, about the work going on in the rabbit warren of rooms at various levels. I remember his remarking to a Canadian research student one day:

"You know, X, I don't believe that you are in and working hard because your hat is hanging behind your door. What have you done this last week or two?"

G. R. CROWE

No proper account of the Cavendish Laboratory under Rutherford could be possible without an appreciation of the part played by G. R. Crowe. Crowe told me that he had been in the Laboratory as an assistant since 1907. Just

42

before the First World War, he became interested in a technical post in New Zealand, and went to Manchester to be interviewed by Rutherford, who had undertaken to select a suitable man. He was not appointed, but after the interview, Rutherford told him that he appreciated the sort of post which Crowe desired, and would bear him in mind if a suitable opening arose. Early in 1919 Crowe was approached by W. L. Bragg, who told him that Rutherford had been appointed as Cavendish Professor and wanted to know whether he was interested to become his personal assistant. Kay, the Laboratory Steward and Lecture Assistant, who had assisted with Rutherford's research in Manchester, was unwilling to migrate to Cambridge. Crowe eagerly agreed, being more attracted by this proposal than by the alternative offer to accompany Bragg to Manchester where he was to succeed Rutherford. Following an interview with Rutherford in London, he was appointed from June, 1919, and worked intimately with "the Prof." as he called him, throughout the remainder of Rutherford's days. One of his first tasks was to go to Manchester to learn how to handle and prepare radio-active sources from radium in solution. The glassware was discoloured and embrittled by exposure to radiation, but it was dismantled, packed, and re-erected under Rutherford's supervision in a small isolated "Tower" room in the Cavendish, without incident. Rutherford had evaporated the radium solution to dryness in Manchester, and he put it into solution again in the Cavendish. From then onward, Crowe regularly pumped off the radon and prepared from it the great variety of radioactive sources required, working under the general supervision of Chadwick, who had accompanied Rutherford from Manchester. He also assisted with the setting up of experiments and the adjustment of apparatus. Crowe tells many stories of Rutherford and Chadwick in those days, some of which have been

43

recorded by Eve and by Cockcroft. He recalls the exuber-
ant excitement of Rutherford when a result of interest was
obtained, and his apprehension when Rutherford took over
any sort of delicate manipulation. For him, he says
nostalgically, those were wonderful days.

In 1926 Crowe became aware that there was something
wrong with the tips of his fingers, with which he handled
radon tubes or manipulated nickel buttons through a
mercury trough into radon collected in a glass tube. He had
been given regular blood tests for the effects of whole body
radiation, but apparently he did not obey the rules laid
down for the preparation and manipulation of sources. In
particular, he did not always wear gloves, preferring to use
his bare fingers. From then, deterioration was rapid, his
fingers and thumbs becoming horny and insensitive, and
painful cracks appeared. Many skin grafts were made and a
finger was amputated. He was withdrawn from work with
radioactive sources, but the damage had been done.
Though severely handicapped, he remained otherwise well
and vigorous, but he had to give up playing the piano, and
his favourite sport of shooting became more difficult.

In 1959, Crowe was retired. He spoke sadly about this for
he was still enjoying his work and, he felt, doing a useful job.
He said:

"It was a Friday, and I walked out of the place as though
I were just going home in the usual way. No-one said
goodbye to me, and even the Professor (W. L. Bragg)
wouldn't have known I was going if I had not gone up to
his office to tell him I was leaving."

Rutherford once said to me, in a moment of exasperation
at some foolish behaviour by a research student, that if the
Laboratory contained 30 Crowes, instead of 30 research
students, a great deal more research would be done. It is sad

44

that one who played so great a part in the wonderful days of Rutherford's period in the Cavendish, should fade from the scene without some ceremonial goodbye. At the instigation of Sir Lawrence Bragg, he was later admitted by the University to the degree of M.A., in recognition of his long and devoted work in the Cavendish Laboratory.

MASS SPECTROSCOPY

F. W. Aston was building a new model of his mass spectograph with greatly improved resolution. He was a lone worker, at that time making very spasmodic appearances in the Laboratory. K. T. Bainbridge, from Harvard, spent a year in Cambridge with the idea of comparing notes and working with Aston on the problems of accurate mass spectrometry, but he made no real contact and gained little from Aston. Aston's laboratory was a dingy, darkened room, in a corner of the ground floor, its walls covered with discarded apparatus and with samples of rare gases in tubes over mercury, which he had separated by fractionating residues from liquid air. He was a good glass-blower and a careful experimenter – Chadwick believes that he was one of the best experimenters he has known. It was thought that he had private means, for although a Fellow of Trinity, he held no University post and made frequent long trips by sea. He was a gifted musician, and in his younger days had excelled in many sports. It was said that when he accompanied a British eclipse expedition to Japan, as an honorary supernumerary, and was given charge of one of the photographic telescopes, he forgot to open the shutter at the critical time. However, I cannot vouch for the truth of that story. He was a bachelor, living in College, and had many of the peculiarities associated with that state. There was a large storage battery in the Cavendish, wired to distribution boards throughout the building. Aston used this to energize the electromagnet of his mass spectrograph. The only time that he was angry with me was an occasion when I was using a crude spark oscillator as an induction heater. Through some misadventure, or because of a resonance in the battery circuit, this caused sparks to pass between the battery terminals in Aston's laboratory. (There were also complaints from Corpus Christi College, across Free School Lane, because of the noise made by the spark gap.)

However, I got on very well with Aston and we often discussed mutual problems of gas discharges and of the difficulties he experienced from electric double layers which formed on the deflecting plates and metal walls of his mass spectrometer. His mass values were of great use to us in early work on artificial disintegration, but later we found inconsistencies among them and showed that, for light elements, we could derive a more consistent mass scale from our measurements of energy. A. E. Kempton, who was working with Rutherford and me, wrote a song which was sung with gusto at the annual Cavendish Dinner, about Aston's hostile reaction to our proposed corrections to his mass values.

Aston was not amused.

THE UPPER FLOOR

On the top floor of the old part of the Cavendish there were a number of small research rooms. The most prominent of those occupying these when I arrived in the Laboratory were N. Feather, E. J. Williams and F. R. Terroux, each working with an expansion chamber.

Norman Feather intrigued us all by his ability to remain neat and clean, with not a hair out of place, whatever he was doing. He had an encyclopaedic knowledge of nuclear

46

physics, was an accomplished experimenter, and shared my deep affection for both Rutherford and Chadwick. E.J. Williams, with a mercurial Welsh temperament, was an extremely good physicist. If he had not died young, he would have made important contributions to physics. Terroux was a Canadian whose gay manner prevented us from becoming too serious.

Many others occupied these rooms during my period in Cambridge, but I saw less of them than I did of those nearer my own place of work.

REFERENCES

1 Sir James Chadwick, "Some Personal Notes on the Search for the Neutron", Ithaca, vol. 26, p. 159 (1962).

CHAPTER 3

Radio, Junk, Tea, Visitors

RADIO

A small group of research workers, headed by J. Ratcliffe, continued investigations of the ionosphere by radio methods, which had been initiated by E. V. Appleton. Occasionally, we heard of this work in excellent lectures by Ratcliffe to the Kapitza Club or the Cavendish Physical Society, but I had no direct contact with it. I do remember a research student, who worked in a room above the Part I Laboratory and who seemed to be interminably engaged in connecting up circuits on a bench. He once explained to me that he carefully thought out where each wire should be connected and screwed or soldered it in position. When the circuit was completed, he went over it again, reversing every pair of leads, certain that it would then be more correctly wired than if left as originally connected! Ratcliffe was a Fellow of Sidney Sussex College, where he had rooms. On the mantel shelf he kept an array of ingenious mechanical puzzles which we attempted to solve on occasions such as a meeting of the Kapitza Club there. He was as fascinated as I was by questions of generation of an e.m.f. in a circuit when either there was no change of flux through the circuit, or there was no cutting of lines of magnetic flux by a moving conductor, and invented a number of models to illustrate the duality of the problem.

In 1936 Appleton returned to Cambridge to succeed

C. T. R. Wilson as Jacksonian Professor of Physics. He gave the first demonstrations of television reception from Alexandra Palace which I had seen, the aerial of the receiving set being at the top of New Court of St. John's College. There was great excitement when he obtained good pictures at about twice the reputed range of the transmitter. Radar, or R.D.F., as it was known originally, was then beginning to show promise. Though he never gave any information of the slightest significance, Appleton obviously enjoyed greatly going off to what he called "hush-hush" meetings in London. By the time that we were initiated into its mysteries in 1939 Appleton had left Cambridge to become Secretary of the Department of Scientific and Industrial Research. He seemed to have been squeezed completely out of radar.

In a ground floor room, through which it was necessary to pass on the way to or from the laboratory occupied by Rutherford and Chadwick, G. I. Taylor worked with a research assistant. He was a remarkable man, probably the last of the universal scientists to which the elder Lord Rayleigh belonged. He had made major contributions to the theory of aerodynamics, and devised simple and most ingenious experiments to demonstrate his conclusions. He was associated with the earliest flight across the Atlantic, from Newfoundland to Britain; had taken part in the design of the airships R 100 and R 101; had used X-rays to study the properties of solids; and had demonstrated that one got the same interference pattern in light from a double slit, at very low intensities, when only a single quantum could be near one of the slits at a given time. He was most kind to me, and infinitely patient in explaining what he was doing to an obviously raw research student.

49

There was a miscellaneous collection of junk in a ground
floor room dignified by being called the store. It was looked
after by a small, elderly man named Rolph, whose main
task, so far as I was concerned, was to fill my vacuum flasks
from a large liquid air container in his keeping. The stores
which most concerned me were kept in cupboards in the
workshop, where Mr. Lincoln presided over a collection of
ancient lathes, milling machines, etc., served by a few
mechanics and apprentices. Lincoln had spent his life in the
Cavendish, and the lean days of former years made him
extremely parsimonious. He was of medium height and
build, carried himself erect, had dark hair and complexion,
and wore a forbidding moustache, waxed to fine points.
If one wanted a length of electrical flex or rubber tubing,
Lincoln measured it out to the inch required. If it was a
piece of "dumet" wire for sealing into glass, tungsten wire
for a filament or pyrex seal, sheet nickel, and so on, he
would almost invariably offer scrap metal in an old
tobacco tin, and only firmness produced virgin material.
He kept these stores in miscellaneous cupboards, securely
locked, but we discovered that when he was not about, it
was possible to unscrew the back and gain illicit access to his
treasures, thus saving a lot of argument. He loved good
timber, and on special occasions could be persuaded to find
"a nice bit of mee'ogany" to mount a piece of apparatus.
Nothing in his store was labelled, but he seldom made a
mistake. On one occasion, however, he wasted some weeks
of my work by giving me a piece of German silver rod which
he swore was pure nickel. Having spent much time shaping
this, drilling it and fitting heaters and thermocouples,
before sealing the whole into a glass bulb, I found to my
consternation that, when heated in vacuum, large quantities of zinc distilled out over walls and electrodes, ruining

the equipment. However, we were all very fond of Lincoln. He trained his boys well, and when I moved to Birmingham he allowed me to take one of them with me, M. P. (Jimmy) Edwards, who remained my gifted assistant till I retired. Lincoln was very proud of his responsibilities, and greatly admired Rutherford, for whom he would click his heels to attention and almost salute, whenever he entered the workshop.

The Cavendish had recently acquired a glass-blower, a Mr. Niedergesass. He was a cadaverous and untidy individual, his fingers yellowed with nicotine, but with uncanny skill in the manipulation of glass. His blowpipes were self-made from glass tubing, pieces of brass, and ordinary corks, and the air to operate them came from a large set of bellows, operated with his foot beneath the bench. Later on, Chadwick, who had persuaded Rutherford to appoint a glass-blower, was able to provide proper equipment, including a glass-blowing lathe. It was a mystery to me how he managed to control a dripping mass of molten glass, and at the same time stand on one leg and pump the bellows with the other. He was both skilful and obliging, with none of the temperamental characteristics of most glass-blowers. He would try anything, no matter how complex, and never complained if I ruined hours of his work by carelessness in handling complicated glassware he had made for me.

The electric supply for Cambridge came from an ancient power station on the bank of the Cam near Magdalene College. It was alternating current at the strange frequency of 93 cycles per second, and at a non-standard 200 volts. This was most awkward, for ordinary commercial equipment could not be used. Most of the motors used in the Laboratory were for direct current at 200 volts obtained from noisy motor-generators in a low building where the Mond Laboratory now stands. However, this had its

51

advantages, for the speed of d.c. motors was easily variable and the supply could be connected directly to electromagnets if some fluctuation in the field could be tolerated. For more stable electromagnets and so on, the large central battery was available, provided that Aston was not using it. In about 1932 the electric supply was changed to 230 volts, 50 cycles, as part of the development of the standard electrical grid for Britain, and the d.c. supplies were then obtained from a rectifier substation. In the late 1920's there were no high voltage supplies in the Laboratory for operating counters etc., such as are standard equipment today. For my work, I was provided with a long box, like a coffin, of polished wood, inside which were several small d.c. generators connected in series and driven by a d.c. motor, the speed of which could be varied by a resistance at one end. It gave an output of about 2,000 volts at full speed, and a few milliamperes of current.

LIBRARY, TEA

There was a small library in the Laboratory where most of the periodicals of importance and a few monographs and books of reference, were available. Books and periodicals could be borrowed overnight, but could not be taken from the library before 4.0 p.m., and had to be returned before 10.0 a.m. next day. There was no librarian on duty, so that borrowers signed their own books out and in. In my experience this worked excellently and few disobeyed the rules. Afternoon tea in a room next to the library was provided in the early 1920's by Lady Rutherford, but when the number of research students increased very rapidly, she provided only the tea, the buns being supplied by members of the Laboratory. This tea break was a valuable institution at which members of the Laboratory chatted together about their work or the weather, but it wasted little time, as there was nowhere to sit down! Sticky Chelsea buns were the favourites at tea. Before the meetings of the Cavendish Physical Society, the tea was provided by the Professor, and Lady Rutherford poured. At these special teas, we got only a half, or even only a quarter of a Chelsea bun! There were more frequent colloquia, attendance at which was confined to graduates. These meetings provided research students with valuable experience in speaking about their work and in the discussion of recent advances in physics. Occasionally, Rutherford invited someone to speak on a subject outside the interest of the Laboratory. I remember one meeting addressed by an expert on the control of the tsetse fly in Africa, whom Rutherford had met on a visit to South Africa.

Hours of work in the section of the Laboratory where I worked initially were from 9.0 a.m. to 6.0 p.m. Only for special reasons would Rutherford allow us to work outside these hours. He explained that the evenings were for reading, writing and, above all, thinking. Promptly at 6.0 p.m., one of the laboratory assistants, Dear, walked round this part of the building pulling out all the main switches. I believe this to have been a very good rule, but sometimes it was enforced with irritating strictness when one was in the middle of an experiment. In other parts of the Cavendish there was greater latitude in hours, and when laboratories such as the Old H. T. Laboratory of Cockcroft, Allibone and Walton were established, the supplies to which were independent of those in the main laboratory, this rule was relaxed completely.

VISITORS TO THE CAVENDISH

There was a constant stream of visitors to the Cavendish,

for at that time it was the recognized centre of research in fundamental physics for the whole world. Of these, the most frequent was Niels Bohr, the distinguished Danish theoretical physicist who had worked with Rutherford for a short time in Manchester, and whose reverence for Rutherford as a physicist was accompanied by a deep and sincere affection for him as a man. Bohr and his charming wife always stayed with the Rutherfords at Newnham Cottage, where my wife and I learned to love them as did Rutherford. Bohr's extraordinary physical insight had developed Rutherford's nuclear atom into a beautiful structure which followed naturally from the necessity to quantize the energies of the outer electrons, and which accounted exactly for the frequencies of the spectral lines emitted when the atom recovered from excited states. His Institute in Copenhagen attracted every ambitious young theoretician, as the Cavendish did experimenters. Almost always he brought new insights into the structure or behaviour of matter or radiation, so that we gathered eagerly to hear what he had to tell us.

Bohr spoke English fluently, but in a peculiar soft, guttural voice, appearing to swallow parts of many words. His wife told us that he spoke Danish in the same manner. While lecturing he was never still, wandering back and forth the whole width of the room or dais, turning at times to write something on the black-board and then his voice became unintelligible. On one occasion when he addressed the Kapitza Club on a hot summer evening, we moved outside to The Backs, and set up a black-board on a slope near the river. When darkness fell, bicycle lamps were used to illuminate the board, but Bohr's perambulations continued, so that he was only spasmodically visible as his path crossed the beam of light, and his voice waxed and waned with the amplitude of his movements. His peculiar English floated to us like that of some disembodied spirit

54

speaking through veils of ectoplasm. He had no sense of time, so that our limbs became cramped from sitting on the grass, and the bicycle lamps grew dim before he stopped at nearly midnight.

The same restless habit made personal discussion with him often difficult, for he would stride about the lawns round his Institute, or at Newnham Cottage, reversing direction unpredictably so that one trotted round him like a puppy. The only occasion when I saw him deprived of the restless walk was when he opened the research laboratories of General Atomics in La Jolla, Southern California. The ceremony took place in the open, and Bohr was provided with a raised pulpit of very small area and surrounded by a battery of microphones! I imagine that he was acutely uncomfortable to find himself caged in this way, but we did have the rare pleasure of hearing all that he said. Of course, when Bohr spoke with Rutherford his mobility was severely restricted, for Rutherford remained obstinately seated.

The gentle Bohr could be obstinate also when he felt that principles were at stake. During the war he and others were smuggled out of German-occupied Denmark to escape imprisonment. He joined the British team working in America on the nuclear weapon. When it became apparent that success was on the way, Bohr was much concerned that the bomb be used as an agent of peace rather than of war. His humanitarian interests were so aroused that he left Los Alamos for Washington, determined to do all in his power to persuade President Roosevelt to use it in this way. During my visits from Oakridge to Washington at this time, to see the leader of our team, Professor James Chadwick, Bohr had many talks with me about what he should say in a letter to the President. He would produce, excitedly, two or three drafts in a day and turn up next morning with still another. In the end he saw Mr. Roosevelt, but not being familiar with Bohr's mannerisms, perhaps the President

55

did not understand at once what he was attempting to say.

Other visitors of note to the Cavendish were Heisenberg, who lectured with great clarity in perfect English; Lise Meitner and Irene Curie-Joliot, women who had made notable contributions to nuclear physics; Geiger, whose counters revolutionized the detection of beta and gamma-rays, as well as cosmic radiation; the extrovert and egotistical Millikan, who had first measured the charge on the electron with precision, which turned out to be much less than he claimed; Ernest Lawrence of cyclotron fame; Langmuir of the G.E. Research Laboratories, Schenectady; Kramers; Basil Schonland from South Africa, who had been a research student with Rutherford and who gave a fascinating talk on lightning; and many others from abroad.

From Britain itself came W. H. and W. L. Bragg, Lord Rayleigh, Oliver Lodge, O. W. Richardson, Charles Darwin, Tyndall, and so on. Indeed, very few of those working in fields in any way related to the work going on in the Cavendish failed to appear at some time.

Blackett, Kapitza, Langevin, Rutherford, C.T.R. Wilson

Einstein and Rutherford, Albert Hall, 1933. Appeal for funds
for the Academic Assistance Council

With Niels Bohr and (l. to r.) Lady Rutherford, Mrs. Oliphant, Mrs. Bohr
1930.

CHAPTER 4

Injustice, History

INJUSTICE AND WAR

In 1933 Hitler's Nazi Regime deprived millions of Jewish Germans of their means of livelihood. Among those displaced were scientists and other intellectuals, many of whom left Germany to swell the multitude of refugees seeking asylum elsewhere. Rutherford was appalled by this brutality, especially as the greatest of the German scientists, some of whom had worked with him and many of whom he knew intimately, were among the victims. In May, 1933, Rutherford was consulted by Beveridge, Trevelyan and Hopkins. In his book, "A defence of Free Learning", Oxford 1959, Lord Beveridge says:

"Most important of all, I persuaded Rutherford, after a first refusal on the ground that he was up to the eyes in other work and against strong opposition by Lady Rutherford, to become President of the Council. .... In the end it was our cause rather than our friendship that brought him over. As we talked, he exploded with wrath at Hitler's treatment of scientific colleagues whom he knew intimately and valued. He would have been miserable not to be with us if we went ahead. He did everything and more to make our going ahead possible."

They produced a draft memorandum conceiving an Academic Assistance Council which would raise a million pounds for the relief of distress among the refugees. Rutherford became President of the Council, funds for which were raised initially through a meeting on 3rd October, 1933, in the Albert Hall, London, at which he presided and made the opening speech to the 10,000 people present. He pointed out the magnitude of the problem, the Academic Assistance Council alone having a list of over a thousand university teachers who had neither income nor the opportunity to carry on with their work:

> "Each of us may have his own private political views, but in this work of relief all such political differences of opinion must give way before the vital necessity of effectively conserving this great body of learning and experience which otherwise will be lost to the world."

Rutherford then introduced the principal speaker and refugee, Albert Einstein, who spoke on "Science and Civilization", carefully avoiding, as had Rutherford, the incitement of nationalist passions:

> " .... It cannot be my task to act as judge of the conduct of a nation which for many years has considered me as her own .... the questions which concern us are: How can we save mankind and its spiritual acquisitions, of which we are the heirs? .... "

In 1934 Rutherford wrote two further appeals for funds, and stressed at all times that the Society must avoid political entanglement of any kind. During this period Paul Harteck was with us. He was Austrian, but had worked with Haber in Berlin. Several times Rutherford asked me whether Harteck had views on the situation of German scientists, particularly as he was not Jewish. He made no secret of his intention not to allow any anti-Jewish sentiments or activities to be spread in the Cavendish. Although, so far as I know, he never expressed his feelings directly to Harteck,

58

who decided to apply for the post in Hamburg which was vacant since Otto Stern had been dismissed, he was distressed by this desire to return to work for the Nazi regime.

Rutherford hated war and violence of every kind, though not to the point of tolerating injustice. In the First World War he had contributed significantly to the development of methods of detecting submerged submarines by observation of sound waves scattered in water from the hull, and of the sound emitted by their engines. His aversion towards the use of scientific knowledge to develop what he regarded as obscene weapons is well illustrated in this letter from Born to Chadwick:

> "Marcardstrasse 4,
> BAD PYRMONT,
> Germany.
> 11 Aug. 1954.

Dear Chadwick,

I have just read your Rutherford Memorial Lecture, 1953, in the number 1159 of Proc. Roy. Soc., which came today, and I wish to tell you how much I enjoyed it. You have given an excellent account of the man and his work. It is one of my most cherished recollections to have known him a little. For he was the greatest man I have met, including even Einstein. There is one point over which I ponder a lot: what would have been his attitude to the present situation of physics in the political world? I remember the following event: when I came to Cambridge in 1933, there was also Fritz Haber, the chemist. He was rather a broken man, deprived of his position, political influence, a honoured but superfluous refugee. I had pity with him and invited him to my house in Hills Road, although I had not been on good terms

with him because I disliked his political and military
activities in the first world war. One day my wife and I
asked Rutherford whether he would like to meet Haber
at a little tea party in my house. He declined violently;
did not wish to have any contact with the man who had
invented chemical warfare with the help of poison-gas.
I have always regarded this statement as a leading help
for myself – until the Nazis perpetrated their crimes and
threatened to subjugate the world. I wonder what
Rutherford himself would have done had he lived to see
the military application of nuclear physics. It is a tragedy
that he cannot show the way. Or should one say that he
was lucky to die before the dilemma arose in its present
magnitude?

Thank you again for that lecture. We have settled here
in a comfortable little house on the foot of lovely hills.
With kind regards,
Yours sincerely,
M. Born"

However, Chadwick has pointed out to me that Rutherford, like most of us, was not very consistent in such
attitudes, for Otto Hahn was also in gas warfare and
Rutherford remained on the most friendly terms with him.

Although the grave menace of Hitler's resurgent
Germany had been recognized by the British Government
when Rutherford died, he did not believe that war would
eventuate. He was an optimist in this, as in almost all
matters.

HISTORY

Rutherford had a keen sense of history, in which he read
widely. He often showed suprising knowledge of the past

in lectures and speeches. Thus in his opening remarks when he received an honorary degree in Göttingen, which are preserved on records, he was able to tell his audience that the University of Göttingen had been founded by George II, King of England, in 1737, ten years after Newton died. In his speech at the Annual Dinner of the Royal Society on 30th November, 1927, Rutherford pointed out that it was just 150 years since Captain Cook had discovered New Zealand, so that if it had not been for Captain Cook, he would not have been presiding at the function that night. This remark stimulated Sir Alfred Yarrow, F.R.S., a generous benefactor of the Royal Society, to send to Rutherford a copy of the entry in the caterers' day book giving details of the food supplied for a luncheon to Captain Cook on board the "Resolution" before his departure for the southern seas, in June, 1776. It is reproduced here. Rutherford was much amused by this and referred several times later to the menu for this light luncheon.

The exploration of the Pacific, especially by Cook, fascinated Rutherford, who had read much about it. On one occasion, he told me in detail what was known at that time of the extensive canoe voyages of the islanders, and of their arrival in New Zealand some 600 years ago.

I remember the glee with which he recounted a story from a book on Frederick the Great, who unified Germany, which he had just read. Frederick was in the habit of entertaining officers from his crack regiment to tea on Sundays. For this function a set of valuable cups and saucers was used. It was found that pieces of this rare porcelain disappeared on each occasion, causing great consternation, until they were discovered on the tops of pieces of furniture where they were not visible to the ordinary eye. Frederick insisted upon tall officers and these men found the tops of bookcases convenient places to deposit their empty cups.

Capt. Cooke, on board the 'Resolution' at Long Reach,
June 8th, 1776

		£ s. d.
	Mr. Smith	
1 Turbot 15s.	3 Trout 15s. 2 Lobsters 2/6	1.12.6
Shrimps 1s.	Basket 6d.	1.6
		£ 1.14.0
	Mr. Boyce	
6 Chickens 12s.	6 Pidgeons 4s.	16.0
	Mr. Trantum	
8 Bottles Strawberries		16.0
	Sundries	
1 Westmorland Ham		12.0
Crusting a pidgeon pye		2.6
1 D. raggooe mellu		5.0
1 D. stew'd mushrooms		5.0
1 D. stew'd peas		3.0
1 D. garden beans		3.0
1 D. Spinage Toasts		6
1 D. Collyflowers		1.0
2 D. Petit patties		3.0
1 neck of Venison		12.0
1 Tart		2.6
1 D. Sweetbreads		7.6
2 lb. Biscuits		4.0
24 French rolls		2.0
Currant jelly, butter, sugar, lemons, charcoal, etc.		4.0
Sauces prepared at home		2.6
Mr. Dignon		1.11.6
Labourer		2.6
Paid a boat with 4 oars to carry provisions, cooks etc. to and from		1.11.6
Fine sugar for fruit		1.0
1 pot gravy		1.0
Porters to the water side		1.0
		£ 6.18.0

	£ s. d.
Dinner	12. 2.0
Disburst	10. 4.0
	£ 1.18.0

The above is a copy of the entry in Messrs. Ring and Brymer's Day Book of the Luncheon given to Captain Cooke on June 8th, 1776, just before his departure for the Far South.

Rutherford was deeply interested in the way in which new concepts were born in science, and for that reason read widely in the biographies of scientists and others, and in such records as Faraday's diaries. Though essentially a modest man, he knew well the significance of his own contributions to science. Even in 1909, following the award of the Nobel Prize, at a dinner given by Manchester University to celebrate the event, J.J. Thomson was able to speak of the sheer genius evident in the work of his remarkable pupil in Montreal, adding:

> "Of all the services that can be rendered to science the introduction of new ideas is the very greatest..... There is nobody who has tested his ideas with more vigour than has Professor Rutherford. There can be no man who more nearly fulfils the design of the founder of the Nobel Prize than he does."*

SENSE OF HUMOUR

Rutherford was easily moved to laughter, but never at the misfortune of others. The infectious roar which he produced was often kindled by his own stories of the ridiculous or of slightly off-beat humour. I remember his telling several times of an occasion early in the century when he and Lady Rutherford were staying with the Duffields** at Glenelg, a sea-coast resort about six miles from

* A. S. Eve, loc. cit.
** Geoffrey Duffield became Professor of Physics in the University of Reading, and later, first Director of Mount Stromlo Observatory in the Australian Capital Territory. He was one of the first to measure gravity at sea, using a sensitive spring balance, made for him by Mr. Littlewood, brother of the distinguished Cambridge mathematician.

Adelaide, in South Australia. Duffield possessed one of the early motor cars in the country. He was driving his guests into Adelaide for a meeting, the Rutherfords in the back seat of the open tourer, and his wife beside him. As they chuffed along, Mrs. Duffield turned back to say excitedly to the passengers:

"Do you know, we've just touched 15 (miles per hour)!" This tale was told with gusto by Rutherford, with minor corrections by his wife, when driving at 50 or more miles per hour on the way to Celyn or Chantry Cottage, the whole car vibrating with his laughter.

It is interesting to recall here that on 6th April, 1910, writing to his mother of his new (and first) motor car, a Wolseley-Siddeley, Rutherford revealed that it was not only the Duffields' car which travelled sedately:

"A car is very easy to manage and far more under control than a horse. We average about 17 miles an hour over country, and on a good road run along freely at 25."

Professor P. I. Dee has recalled for me a story in different vein, as follows:

"One story you probably cannot repeat, I didn't dare to do so in the R.S., was a private joke he had with me. Often he would make suggestions about things on (expansion chamber) photographs of a rather wild character. Often I had to show him that these strange effects were readily explained by the nature of the condensation process or the denuding of H_2O in some areas by previous tracks or ion movement etc. This always amused him a lot and he said I reminded him of a man who went to the police because he said a neighbour used to "pee" his daughter's name on the wall! The police asked, 'How do you know it is A who does this?' The man replied: 'I recognize the handwriting!' Often

RUTHERFORD AND J.J. THOMSON

At the Cavendish, 1935

Watching cricket, 1936

Kapitza and Chadwick.
Dressed for Chadwick's wedding

Rutherford at the weel of his first motor car

later R. would say to me, sometimes in company, 'Ah, you recognize the handwriting eh?' and roar with laughter at the private joke!"

On Sunday nights, Rutherford dined regularly in Trinity College and often returned with a tale which he had heard at High Table, or in the Combination Room afterwards. I have heard from those who were present how his laughter stopped all other conversation with its contagious volume. If it was anything like that with which he repeated the tale, its effect must have been devastating.

Rutherford was not altogether a pragmatist, though he generally took a very practical view of nature. Thus, in responding to the toast, "Science", proposed on 30th April, 1932, by the President of the Royal Academy of Arts, he said:

".... Art flowered long before science or the scientific method had taken root. .... Yet I think that a strong claim can be made that the process of scientific discovery may be regarded as a form of art. This is best seen in the theoretical aspects of Physical Science. The mathematical theorist builds up on certain assumptions and according to well understood logical rules, step by step, a stately edifice, while his imaginative power brings out clearly the hidden relation between its parts. A well constructed theory is in some respects undoubtedly an artistic production. A fine example is the famous Kinetic Theory of Maxwell, the centenary of whose birth we celebrated last year. The theory of relativity by Einstein, quite apart from any question of its validity, cannot but be regarded as a magnificent work of art...

I should like to mention one case where the artist – quite unknowingly – has been able to provide valuable data for science. The clay from which the Greek potter made his beautiful vases more than 2000 years ago

65

always contained some magnetic oxide of iron. At a certain stage of the cooling, after firing, the iron particles are very susceptible to the action of magnetic forces, and orient themselves in the direction of the earth's magnetic field. The direction of this magnetisation was fixed permanently when the vase cooled and since we know the vase must have been always in a vertical position during the firing, the scientific man can find the direction of this magnetisation and thus fix the inclination or 'dip' of the earth's magnetic field at the time and for the place where the vase was made. By this curious observation we have been able to extend our knowledge of the secular variations in the earth's magnetic field to a remote epoch more than 2000 years before the importance of such measurements was recognised....

.... (This) is a time of intense intellectual activity, rich in the development of new ideas and methods. For nearly three centuries this country has produced its full quota of great pioneers both in pure and applied science and it still continues to do so. Quite recently there has been much interest taken by the cultivated public in the metaphysical aspects of science, especially those of theoretical physics. Some of our publicists have boldly claimed that the old ideas which served science so well in the past must be abandoned for an ideal world where the law of causality fails, and the principle of uncertainty, so valuable in the proper domain of atomic physics, is pushed to extremes. The great army in its march into the unknown discusses with interest, and sometimes amusement, these fine spun disputations of what is reality and what is truth. But it still goes marching on, calling out to the metaphysicians 'there are more things in heaven and earth than are dreamt of in your philosophy'."

66

CHAPTER 5

Chadwick and the Neutron

CHADWICK

In my time, Chadwick was Rutherford's lieutenant in the running of the Cavendish. He had worked with Rutherford in Manchester, and moved with him to Cambridge. He was most conscientious in his duties and knew more intimately than Rutherford just what every person in the Laboratory was doing. It was Chadwick who saw that research students got the equipment they needed, within the very limited resources of the stores and funds at his disposal. It was he who trained raw recruits to research in a "kindergarten" laboratory in a loft above Rutherford's office. With Rutherford, he chose the research tasks of most students and set them on their way. He read and criticized the papers they wrote. It was Chadwick who organized colloquia and arranged that the Annual Dinner took place at the appropriate time. Rutherford was a mighty leader, but he made full use of his lieutenants in the task. His commitments outside the Laboratory could never have been satisfied without Chadwick's continued, unselfish attention. There were others upon whom Rutherford unloaded some of his responsibilities – later on Ellis, Cockcroft and I became involved. But no-one else bore anything like the burden carried by Chadwick, and no-one else played so vital a part in the initiation and direction of the research work.

Chadwick read all the journals and knew everything which happened in branches of physics of interest in the Cavendish. If something appeared which seemed worth following up, it was not long before someone in the Laboratory was working on it. The manner in which Bothe's observation of penetrating gamma-rays produced from beryllium bombarded by alpha-particles led to the discovery of the neutron, is one good illustration of such awareness and follow-up. Another was an article by Davis in the Physical Review, claiming that alpha-particles captured more easily electrons travelling with them in the same direction and with the same velocities. Chadwick got de Bruyne, who had been working on the strong-field emission of electrons from metals, and was therefore familiar with vacuum and electron acceleration techniques, to repeat the observations. De Bruyne showed conclusively that the published results were erroneous, and that a resonance capture at zero relative velocity needed to be many orders of magnitude greater in probability than any reasonable theory would permit, at very large distances, to give any detectable effect.

One way in which Chadwick was of immense help to us all, was through his remarkable critical faculty. Shoddy work or loose thinking could not pass the fine filter of his criticism. His clear-headedness prevented him from being carried away by evanescent enthusiasms, as was I. He seldom claimed any credit for his major part in much of the most important work done in the Laboratory. Under his guidance many young men achieved reputations which were not wholly deserved, as was shown when they moved away from his tutelage.

To the young research student, Chadwick seemed generally dour and unsmiling, and it took some time before the kindly, helpful and generous person beneath became apparent. He was Rutherford's closest collaborator and colleague in the Cavendish period. His respect and deep love for Rutherford are apparent in the words he wrote in "Nature" for 30th October, 1937, shortly after Rutherford's death:

"Even the casual reader of Rutherford's papers must be deeply impressed by his power in experiment. One experiment after the other is so directly conceived, so clean and so convincing as to produce a feeling almost of awe, and they come in such profusion that one marvels that one man could do so much. He had, of course, a volcanic energy and an intense enthusiasm – his most obvious characteristic – and an immense capacity for work. A 'clever' man with these advantages can produce notable work, but he would not be a Rutherford. Rutherford had no cleverness – just greatness. He had the most astonishing insight into physical processes, and in a few remarks he would illuminate a whole subject. There is a stock phrase – 'to throw light on a subject'. This is exactly what Rutherford did. To work with him was a continual joy and wonder. He seemed to know the answer before the experiment was made, and was ready to push on with irresistible urge to the next. He was indeed a pioneer – a word he often used – at his best in exploring an unknown country, pointing out the really important features and leaving the rest for others to survey at leisure. He was, in my opinion, the greatest experimental physicist since Faraday.

I cannot end this tribute to Rutherford without some words about his personal qualities. He knew his worth but he was and remained, amidst his many honours, innately modest. Pomposity and humbug he disliked, and he himself never presumed on his reputation or position. He treated his students, even the most junior, as brother workers in the same field – and when necessary spoke to them 'like a father'. These virtues, with his large, generous nature and his robust common sense, endeared him to all his students. All over the world workers in radioactivity, nuclear physics and allied subjects regarded Rutherford as the great authority and paid him tribute of high admiration; but we, his students, bore him also a very deep affection. The world mourns the death of a great scientist, but we have lost our friend, our counsellor, our staff and our leader."

THE NEUTRON

In his Bakerian Lecture to the Royal Society on 3rd June, 1920, Rutherford spoke of the constitution of the nuclei of atoms, describing experiments on the disintegration of nitrogen and oxygen by bombardment with alpha-particles in which a particle of mass 3 and charge 2 appeared to be produced. It was assumed, tentatively, that this particle must have been a constituent of the nuclei from which it escaped. He went on to say:[1]

"In his recent experiments on the isotopes of ordinary elements Aston[2] has shown that within the limit of experimental accuracy the masses of all isotopes examined are given by whole numbers when oxygen is taken as 16. The only exception is hydrogen, which has a mass 1.008, in agreement with chemical observations. This does not exclude the probability that hydrogen is the ultimate constituent of which nuclei are composed, but indicates that either the grouping of the hydrogen nuclei and electrons is such that the average electromagnetic mass is nearly 1, or, what is more probable, that the secondary units, of which the atom is mainly built up, e.g., helium or its isotope, have a mass given nearly by a whole number when O is 16.

70

The experimental observations made so far are unable to settle whether the new atom has a mass exactly 3, but from the analogy with helium we may expect the nucleus of the new atom to consist of three H nuclei and one electron and to have a mass more nearly 3 than the sum of the individual masses in the free state.

If we are correct in this assumption it seems very likely that one electron can also bind two H nuclei and possibly also one H nucleus. In the one case, this entails the possible existence of an atom of mass nearly 2 carrying one charge, which is to be regarded as an isotope of hydrogen. In the other case, it involves the idea of the possible existence of *an atom of mass 1 which has zero nucleus charge*.* Such an atomic structure seems by no means impossible. On present views, the neutral hydrogen atom is regarded as a nucleus of unit charge with an electron attached at a distance, and the spectrum of hydrogen is ascribed to the movements of this distant electron. Under some conditions, however, it may be possible for an electron to combine much more closely with the H nucleus, forming a kind of neutral doublet. Such an atom would have very novel properties. Its external field would be practically zero, except very close to the nucleus, and in consequence it should be able to move freely through matter. Its presence would probably be difficult to detect by the spectroscope, and it may be impossible to contain it in a sealed vessel. On the other hand, it should enter readily the structure of atoms, and may either unite with the nucleus or be disintegrated by its intense field, resulting possibly in the escape of a charge H atom or an electron or both.

If the existence of such atoms be possible, it is to be expected that they may be produced, but probably only

* My italics – M.L.O.

in very small numbers in the electric discharge through hydrogen, where both electrons and H nuclei are present in considerable numbers. It is the intention of the writer to make experiments to test whether any indication of the production of such atoms can be obtained under these conditions.

The existence of such nuclei may not be confined to mass 1 but may be possible for masses 2, 3 or 4, or more, depending on the possibility of combination between the doublets. The existence of such atoms seems almost necessary to explain the building up of the nuclei of heavy elements; for unless we suppose the production of charged particles of very high velocities it is difficult to see how any positively charged particle can reach the nucleus of a heavy atom against its intense repulsive field."

At about the same time, Harkins[3] discussed the constitution of nuclei mainly from the point of view of their masses and arrangement in orderly series. He too assumed that an electron or electrons could be bound tightly to a proton or helium nucleus (nu particles) to form the constituent bricks from which all nuclei are built. However, he does not appear to have appreciated the properties of the neutron as did Rutherford, though, so far as I can discover, he was the first to publish the word "neutron".

Chadwick has given an account[4] of the search for the neutron which followed the remarkable hypothesis which Rutherford had put forward. With characteristic modesty, Chadwick does not make it clear that while Rutherford never lost his deep interest in the search for the neutron, it was the persistence of Chadwick, who followed up every possible indication, which finally brought success. He wrote:

".... I believe that only on one occasion after the Bakerian Lecture did he (Rutherford) again refer

72

publicly to his views on the role of the neutron. He had not abandoned the idea, and he had completely converted me. From time to time in the course of the following years, sometimes together, sometimes myself alone, we made experiments to find evidence of the neutron, both its formation and its emission from atomic nuclei."

The earliest of these experiments were made by J. L. Glasson[5] using a beam of positive ions of hydrogen striking a lead target, and a little later J. K. Roberts looked calorimetrically for the missing energy due to the production of neutrons when an electric discharge was passed through hydrogen. Roberts and I worked for a time in the same room, and during intervals in our experiments he told me of this work:

"A crazy idea of the Prof. or Chadwick on which I wasted a lot of time."

This conversation took place in 1931. Chadwick thought that if a close combination of proton and electron were possible, it might occur spontaneously in hydrogen. Rutherford agreed that the experiment should be tried, so in 1923 Chadwick looked without success for gamma-radiation which could be produced in the process of combination, using an ionization chamber and a point counter as detectors. Following the invention by Geiger and Müller of far more sensitive counters, in 1928, Rutherford and Chadwick looked for spontaneously produced radiation from hydrogen, the rare gases, and a number of rare elements, but found nothing.

Chadwick also thought it worth examining whether protons accelerated to 200,000 eV could unite with the tightly bound inner electrons of the heavy elements. He carried out some experiments using Tesla voltages, but the equipment and techniques available in the Cavendish at that time were inadequate.

Of experiments which it is now known might have

provided evidence for the existence of the elusive particle, Chadwick has written:*

"During our work on the disintegration of the lighter elements by alpha-particles Rutherford and I had not been unmindful of the possibility of the emission of neutrons, especially from those elements which did not emit protons. We looked for faint scintillations due to a radiation undeflected by a magnetic field. The only specific reference to the search for the neutron in this way was made in a paper published in 1929, some years after the experiments.

The case of beryllium was interesting for two reasons.

It did not emit protons under alpha-particle bombardment; and, though a false argument, the mineral beryl was known to contain an unusual amount of helium suggesting that perhaps the Be nucleus split up under the action of the cosmic radiation into two alpha-particles and a neutron.

This matter intrigued me on and off for some years. I bombarded beryllium with alpha-particles, with beta-particles and with gamma-rays, generally using the scintillation method to detect any effect. In those days this was the only method of much use in the presence of the strong gamma radiation of the radium active deposit, the chief source of radiation available to me. Quite early on, too early perhaps, I tried to devise suitable electrical methods of counting. I failed. Later, when the valve amplifier method had been developed by Greinacher, and put into use in the Cavendish by Wynn-Williams, I was also able to make a polonium source, small but just enough for the purpose. With Constable and Pollard, I had another look at beryllium, and for a short but exciting time we thought we had found some evidence of the neutron.

* Sir James Chadwick, loc. cit.

74

But somehow the evidence faded away. I was still groping in the dark."

Chadwick set H.C. Webster, an Australian research student, to work examining the gamma-radiation produced by alpha-particle bombardment of beryllium, using a Geiger counter as detector. When a polonium source of much greater intensity became available, through Dr. N. Feather, from old radon tubes from the Kelly Hospital in Baltimore, Webster observed that the radiation from beryllium emitted in the forward direction was more penetrating than that emitted backwards. Chadwick wrote:*

"This fact, clearly established, excited me; it could only be readily explained if the radiation consisted of particles, and, from its penetrating power, of neutral particles."

However, in June, 1931, Webster and Champion were unable to obtain any tracks in an expansion chamber which would verify the supposition. Then, one morning, Chadwick read:

".... the communication of the Curie-Joliots in the *Comptes Rendus*, in which they reported a still more surprising property of the radiation from beryllium that of ejecting protons from matter containing hydrogen, a most startling property. Not many minutes afterwards Feather came to my room to tell me about this report, as astonished as I was. A little later that morning I told Rutherford. It was a custom of long standing that I should visit him about 11.0 a.m., to tell him any news of interest and to discuss the work in progress in the laboratory. As I told him about the Curie-Joliot observation and their views on it, I saw his growing amazement; and finally he

* Sir James Chadwick, loc. cit.

75

burst out, 'I don't believe it'. Such an impatient remark was utterly out of character, and in all my long association with him I recall no similar occasion. I mention it to emphasize the electrifying effect of the Curie-Joliot report. Of course, Rutherford agreed that one must believe the observations; the explanation was quite another matter.

It so happened that I was just ready to begin experiment, for I had prepared a beautiful source of polonium from the Baltimore material. I started with an open mind, though naturally my thoughts were on the neutron. I was reasonably sure that the Curie-Joliot observations could not be ascribed to a kind of Compton effect, for I had looked for this more than once. I was convinced that there was something quite new as well as strange. A few days of strenuous work were sufficient to show that these strange effects were due to a neutral particle and to enable me to measure its mass: the neutron postulated by Rutherford in 1920 had at last revealed itself."

Thus, the neutron was discovered as a result of a persistent search by Chadwick, and not by accident, as were radioactivity and X-rays. Chadwick felt intuitively that it must exist and never gave up the chase. In this, and in other matters, such as the realization for the first time that a fast neutron chain-reaction was possible, and hence a nuclear weapon could be made, Chadwick exhibited much of the insight into the properties of nuclei which made Rutherford so outstanding.

I remember vividly the occasion when Chadwick described his experiments to the Kapitza Club. He had been dined and wined well by Kapitza beforehand, in celebration of the discovery, and was in a very mellow mood. The intense excitement of all in the Cavendish, including Rutherford, was already remarkable, for we had heard rumours of Chadwick's results. His account of the experiments was extremely lucid and convincing, and the ovation he received from his audience was spontaneous and warm. All enjoyed the story of a long quest, carried through with such persistence and vision, and they rejoiced in the success of a colleague. Chadwick's meticulous recognition of the parts played by Webster, by Bothe and Becker, and by Curie-Joliot, in pointing the way, was a lesson to us all.

REFERENCES

1 Lord Rutherford, Proc. Roy, Soc., vol. 97, p. 395 (1920).
2 F.W. Aston, Phil. Mag., vol. 38, p. 707 (1919); vol. 39, p. 449 (1920); vol. 39, p. 611 (1920).
3 W. D. Harkins, Phys. Rev., vol. 15, p. 73 (1920) and other papers.
4 Sir James Chadwick, Ithaca, vol. 26, p. 159 (1962).
5 J.L. Glasson, Phil. Mag., vol. 42, p. 596 (1921).

CHAPTER 6

Cockcroft and Walton

The first member of the Cavendish Laboratory whom I got to know well was John Cockcroft. He had come up to St. John's College in 1922, a more mature student than most, with experience at the University of Manchester, the Manchester College of Technology under Miles Walker, and at the Metropolitan Vickers Electrical Company in Manchester. His family owned a small cotton mill in Todmorden. He had done brilliantly in the Mathematics Tripos and joined the Cavendish Laboratory as a research student in 1925. When we met he and I were both married, and they had a baby son. They lived in a new house which they had built recently in Sedley Taylor Road, the glass of the bay window in the living room being a special variety which transmitted ultra-violet radiation, believed to be beneficial for a young child. The two families became firm friends, the baby being a special attraction for my wife, who loved very young children.

At the time, Cockcroft was doing some work on the properties of thin films deposited on polished, outgassed surfaces, using the best vacuum technique then available. The "housekeeper" type copper-to-glass seals which provided the deposition chamber of his apparatus, were made for him by a remarkable glassblower in Bristol University, but repeated heating to outgas, followed by cooling to liquid nitrogen temperatures, caused them to give trouble. I also was preparing to work with evacuated

78

apparatus, so we found much of interest to discuss. His equipment was set up in a semi-basement room beyond the Part I Laboratory, adjacent to Physical Chemistry, which he shared with T. E. Allibone and E. T. S. Walton, a newcomer. Allibone had some previous experience of high voltage work in the Research Laboratories of Metropolitan Vickers. When I arrived in the Cavendish he had set up a Tesla coil giving a peak potential of several hundreds of thousands of volts, which he applied across a pair of hollow electrodes in a long evacuated glass tube with an elliptical bulb blown at the centre, an experiment suggested by C. D. Ellis, based on the work of A. S. Coolidge. His vacuum system employed an oil diffusion pump recently developed by Burch. This was my first contact with such pumps which so greatly simplified the problem of evacuating relatively large volumes at high speed. Allibone used his apparatus to accelerate electrons, which passed through a thin window into the air beneath. There, he was able to produce brilliant luminescence in a variety of colours by allowing the electrons to impinge upon mineral specimens.

Walton had accepted Rutherford's suggestion to try to accelerate electrons inductively with a varying magnetic field. His small glass apparatus, surrounded by a solenoid, did not satisfy the stability conditions afterwards laid down by Kerst, so he was not successful. He then attempted to make a high frequency linear accelerator like the X-ray device of Sloan and Lawrence, with no more success.

These early experiments of Allibone and Walton were made in response to Rutherford's desire to have at his disposal, for work on nuclear disintegration, far more intense beams of bombarding particles than the alpha particles from radioactive sources were capable of providing.

Chadwick had urged Rutherford, from 1922 on, to establish work in the Cavendish on the acceleration of particles with high voltages. Rutherford did appear to be much interested, but five years later, he said in his Anniversary Address as President of the Royal Society on 30th November, 1927:

"In the short time at my disposal, I would like to make a few remarks on the results of investigations carried out in recent years to produce .... high voltages for general scientific purposes. ....

There appears to be no obvious limit to the voltages obtainable by the cascade arrangement of transformers, except that of expense and the size of the building required to install them. I am informed that the General Electric Company of Schenectady have a working plant giving 2,800,000 volts (max.) and hope soon to have ready a plant to give 6 million volts.

While no doubt the development of such high voltages serves a useful technical purpose, from the purely scientific point of view interest is mainly centred on the application of these high potentials to vacuum tubes in order to obtain a copious supply of high-speed electrons and high-speed atoms. So far we have not yet succeeded in approaching, much less surpassing, the success of the radioactive elements, in providing us with high-speed α-particles and swift electrons. The α-particle from radium C is liberated with an energy of 7.6 million electron volts, i.e., it has the energy acquired by an electron in a vacuum which has fallen through this difference of potential. The swiftest β-rays from radium have an energy of about 3 million electron volts, while a voltage of more than 2 million would be required to produce X-rays of the penetrating power of the γ-rays....

Taking advantage of the great improvements in vacuum technique and the ease of supply of electrons from a glowing filament, Dr. Coolidge has constructed

Cockcroft in the Cavendish, circa 1930

Kapitza beside his heavy current machine

THE MOND LABORATORY

The crocodile

Ruthermond!

an electron tube which will stand 300,000 volts, the rays passing into the air through a thin plate of chrome-nickel-iron alloy about 0.0005 inch thick.

It has not so far been found practicable to apply much more than 300,000 volts to a single tube, on account of the danger of a flash over, due possibly to the pulling-out of electrons from the cathode by the intense electric field. For the application of still higher voltages, a number of tubes are arranged in series and communicating with one another, the fall of potential in each being about 300,000 volts. In these preliminary experiments, a large induction coil has been used to generate the voltage. So far experiments have been made with three tubes in series and 900,000 volts, giving a supply of electrons corresponding to one or two milliamperes through the thin window in the last tube. This gives an intense beam of high-velocity electrons, which spreads out into a hemisphere, due to the scattering of the electrons in passing through the metal window and the surrounding air, extending to a distance of about two metres from the window. Marked luminous effects are produced in the air itself and in phosphorescent bodies placed in the path of the rays. I am informed by Dr. Coolidge that further experiments are in progress and it is hoped to extend the system for still higher voltages.

While the energy acquired by the individual electrons in falling through 900,000 volts is smaller than that possessed by the swifter ß-particles expelled from radium, the number emitted from the electron tube is very much greater; for example, the number of electrons per second corresponding to a current of 2 milliamperes is equivalent to the number of ß-rays emitted per second from about 150,000 grammes of radium in equilibrium.

While important progress has been made in artificially producing streams of swift electrons, there is still much work to be done before we can hope to produce streams of atoms and electrons of a much higher individual energy than the α or ß-particle spontaneously liberated from radioactive bodies. As we have seen the α-particle from radium C is initially expelled with an energy of about 8 million electron volts. So far the α-particle has the greatest individual energy of any particle known to science, and for this reason it has been invaluable in exploring the inner structure of the atom and giving us important data on the magnitude of the deflecting field in the neighbourhood of atomic nuclei and of the dimensions of the nuclei. In case of some of the lighter atoms, the α-particle has sufficient energy to penetrate deeply into the nucleus and to cause its disintegration manifested by the liberation of swift protons.

It would be of great scientific interest if it were possible in laboratory experiments to have a supply of electrons and atoms of matter in general, of which the individual energy of motion is greater even than that of the α-particle. This would open up an extraordinarily interesting field of investigation which could not fail to give us information of great value, not only on the constitution and stability of atomic nuclei but in many other directions.

It has long been my ambition to have available for study a copious supply of atoms and electrons which have an individual energy far transcending that of the α and β-particles from radioactive bodies. I am hopeful that I may yet have my wish fulfilled, but it is obvious that many experimental difficulties will have to be surmounted before this can be realised, even on a laboratory scale."

Late in 1929, the Russian theoretical physicist, Gamow, visited the Cavendish. He had been working with Bohr in Copenhagen, and had developed a wave-mechanical theory of penetration of particles through, rather than over, a potential barrier, which gave an excellent picture of alpha-particle emission and of the reverse penetration of energetic charged particles into an atomic nucleus. Gurney and Condon had developed similar ideas in U.S.A. Cockcroft was quick to realize that this model enabled calculations to be made of the possibility of producing nuclear disintegrations in light atoms by bombarding them with artificially accelerated protons. He estimated, from Gamow's theory, that a beam of a microampere of protons, impinging on boron with an energy of some hundreds of thousands of electron-volts, could produce several millions of disintegrations per minute. Rutherford was sufficiently impressed to allow Cockcroft to go ahead. Walton, disappointed by his unsuccessful attempts to produce fast particles, joined Cockcroft. With a miscellaneous collection of bits and pieces, they assembled a voltage-doubling rectifying circuit, which they connected with an evacuated accelerating tube of the type developed by Allibone, but using a canal-ray source of hydrogen ions in place of the electron emitter. They obtained erratic beams of a few microamperes and bombarded elements from all parts of the periodic table, looking for the gamma-radiation which might result from capture of a proton. They observed some very absorbable radiation in the soft X-ray or ultra-violet region, but no gamma-rays of the very high energy expected, since 5–10 MeV of mass-energy should become available upon capture of a proton by a nucleus.

It is fortunate that, in the middle of 1931, Cockcroft and Walton had to dismantle their apparatus, as their semi-basement laboratory had been transferred to the physical chemists. They moved into a much larger room, with a high ceiling, which had been a lecture theatre. This provided the opportunity to start again from scratch, using an ingenious voltage multiplying circuit which Cockcroft had developed, and which they had tested out at low voltages with ordinary radio-receiver rectifiers and capacitors. They constructed a voltage quadrupling system using this new circuit. The rectifiers were built in glass cylinders, some three or four feet long and 15 inches in diameter, mounted one above the other, the whole stack of four tubes being evacuated at the bottom end with an oil diffusion pump. The intermediate electrodes were pieces of thin-walled steel tubing fitted with rounded steel ends. The top electrode of each pair carried a hairpin shaped tungsten wire filament, which was heated by lead batteries standing on tall insulated stands. The glass tubes were separated by sheets of galvanized iron, and the vacuum joints between these sheets and the glass were made by pressing into the angle a low vapour-pressure plasticine developed by Burch. They had many difficulties before the system became vacuum-tight, and then began the slow, tedious process of clean-up. The applied voltage was raised slowly till a glow-discharge began, when it was reduced to zero. This cycle was repeated over many hours, each time raising the voltage at which break-down occurred. At last, the system would operate continuously without the rectifiers going soft, the top of the stack now being at a steady positive potential of 500 or 600 kilovolts. There was much corona, and if the rectifier filament emission saturated, copious X-rays were produced.

The voltage from this circuit was applied to a two-stage accelerating tube, constructed and evacuated in the same manner as the rectifier stack. A small glass canal-ray tube at the top was energized from a small alternator, driven by a long belt, together with a transformer and rectifier.

There were frequent vacuum troubles due to heat softening the plasticine, or to puncturing of one of the glass cylinders by a spark. Cockcroft and Walton spent a large part of their time perched on ladders, locating and repairing such leaks, or just rubbing over every plasticine joint with their fingers in the hope that they would eventually make the system vacuum-tight again.

In a letter to me, Walton has written of their work:

"By December 1931 the rectifiers and accelerating tube were in reasonable working order and during the next few months we made measurements on the range of the protons in air and checked their velocity by magnetic deflection. The latter gave information about the ratio of protons to molecular ions in the beam. January to March 1932 seems to have been spent on such work. This was interrupted by various troubles and by construction work on a new accelerating tube in March. As late as 12th April, we were still making some measurements on magnetically deflected beams."

Rutherford was impatient while these experiments were being done. He was not interested in the technique, but wanted to know whether the beam could produce any nuclear effects. Walton goes on to say:

"We then put in a lithium target and placed a willemite screen inside the vacuum. As you have asked for particulars of finding the first disintegrations, I will put down my recollections in some detail.

On Thursday, 13th April, I carried out the usual daily conditioning of the apparatus during which Cockcroft was not present in the room. He was doing something for Kapitza in the magnetic lab. When the voltage and the current of protons reached a reasonably high value, I decided to have a look for scintillations. So I left the control table while the apparatus was running and I crawled over to the hut under the accelerating tube. Immediately I saw scintillations on the screen. I then went back to the control table and switched off the power to the proton source. On returning to the hut, no scintillations could be seen. After a few more repetitions of this kind of thing, I became convinced that the effect was genuine. Incidentally, these were the first α-particle scintillations I had ever seen and they fitted in with what I had read about them. I then 'phoned Cockcroft who came immediately. He had a look at the scintillations and after repeating my observations, he also was convinced of their genuine character. He then rang up Rutherford who arrived shortly afterwards. With some difficulty we manoeuvered him into the rather small hut and he had a look at the scintillations. He shouted out instructions such as, 'Switch off the proton current'; 'Increase the accelerating voltage' etc., but he said little or nothing about what he saw. He ultimately came out of the hut, sat down on a stool and said something like this: 'Those scintillations look mighty like α-particle ones. I should know an α-particle scintillation when I see one for I was in at the birth of the α-particle and I have been observing them ever since.' I have since thought that he might have added that he was also in on their christening! He did not stay very long but came back next day and did some scintillation counting. He did about a dozen counts of which the details are in my notebook.

During his visit on 14th April, Rutherford swore us both to strict secrecy and this surprised me at the time. It was a wise precaution as it enabled us to get a lot of work done quickly without any interruption from visitors. By working late in the evenings we soon accumulated essential information about the disintegrations and by Saturday evening, 16th April, we had even seen the tracks of the particles in an expansion chamber. At about 9 or 10 o'clock that evening, we went round to Rutherford's house to report on the results and a letter to 'Nature' was drawn up there."

Cockcroft and Walton correctly interpreted their observation as due to the transformation of the lithium isotope of mass 7 into two alpha-particles, and showed that the energy release was in good accord with the known masses of the hydrogen atom, the helium atom and the lithium 7 atom, as measured by Aston, assuming the validity of Einstein's mass-energy relation, $E = mc^2$.

Rutherford was elated by this discovery, as were all members of the Laboratory. When, shortly afterwards, it was announced publicly at a meeting of the Royal Society, it caused great excitement throughout the world. Thus was initiated the age of particle accelerators in nuclear physics. E. O. Lawerence, in U.S.A., whose cyclotron had come into successful operation, at once showed that this instrument, with its higher beam energy, was a very powerful tool for use in this new field of investigation. Accelerators grew at an amazing pace in laboratories in America, Europe and even in Japan.

Of some inconsistencies between Cockcroft's notes and published accounts, Walton wrote to me:

"I know very little about any records which Cockcroft may have compiled. There is only a hazy recollection in my mind of seeing him on a few occasions writing up a notebook. During the period when we were using the mechanical oscillograph to record the emission of α-particles and protons, I usually took the photographic strips (often wet!) home with me and I would analyse them at night. I would have the results worked out and entered into my notebook along with relevant graphs in time for discussion the following morning. I remember on one occasion, Cockcroft asked me to read out the figures so that he could have a copy for himself. Thereupon I made a good resolution to take a carbon copy for J.D.C. of any tables which I drew up in rough form before entering them in my notebook. I can't remember for how long I kept this up!"

Dr. W.B. Lewis has drawn my attention to a brochure written by Sir Arthur Eddington in 1935, in support of an appeal for funds for the Cavendish Laboratory. In this Eddington says of the work of Cockcroft and Walton:

"Many important developments of this work have followed in the Cavendish, in Paris, in Rome and elsewhere. The 250 isotopes which correspond to stable atoms have been augmented by a great number of temporary atoms artificially created – jerry-built structures which break down in a few minutes or hours. Most important is the insight into the structure of the nucleus that results. We only really understand the working of a machine if we can take it to pieces; and that is what we are now able to do with the atomic nucleus. Splitting the once 'indivisible atom' has become the ordinary occupation of the physicist since 1932.

   The social unsettlement of the age has extended to the world of atoms. An atom which for the last thousand million years has lived peacefully as silicon may tomorrow find itself phosphorus."

On 2nd May, 1932, Bohr replied as follows to a letter from Rutherford telling him of the exciting developments:*

"By your kind letter with the information about the wonderful new results arrived in your laboratory you made me a very great pleasure indeed. Progress in the field of nuclear constitution is at the moment really so rapid, that one wonders what the next post will bring, and the enthusiasm of which every line in your letter tells will surely be common to all physicists. One sees a broad

* A.S. Eve, loc. cit.

88

new avenue opened, and it should soon be possible to predict the behaviour of any nucleus under given circumstances. When one learns that protons and lithium nuclei simply combine into alpha particles, one feels that it could not
have been different although nobody has ventured to think
so. Perhaps more than ever I wish in these days, that I
was not so far away from you and the Cavendish
Laboratory, but the more thankful I am for your kind
communication and the more eager to learn about any
further progress. ...."

CHAPTER 7

The Crocodile

The most colourful figure in the Cavendish when I
arrived was Peter Kapitza. He had suffered greatly during
the communist rebellion and its aftermath, when he lost his
first wife and family. A trained engineer, he had been sent
to Britain shortly after the end of the 1914–1918 War to
purchase scientific equipment. He had visited the Cavendish with Joffe, admired Rutherford greatly, and was
aware of the outstanding reputation of the Cavendish
Laboratory as a centre of research. Like Rutherford at the
same age, he was confident of his own ability, and was keen
to follow a career in research. So, without false modesty he
approached Rutherford, seeking the opportunity to work
with him. He was admitted as a research student by
Rutherford in July, 1921.

> "12a Langham Mansions,
> Earls Court Square,
> London. S.W.5.

Dear Sir Ernest,
  Please let me tell you once more how very grateful I am
to you of having admitted me among your pupils. I hope
to do my best to profit my staying in Cambridge and the
honour to be under your rule.
  If you don't object I will come to Cambridge this
Thursday and take up my work at once.
> Yours truly, Pierre Kapitza"

Kapitza has recollected[1] that on the day that he began work in the Cavendish, Rutherford suddenly declared that he would not allow communist propaganda in the Laboratory.

Kapitza proved himself so energetic, and so fertile of bold ideas that he made spectacular progress. By 1925 he had been elected a Fellow of Trinity College, and in 1929 he became a Fellow of the Royal Society, an unprecedented honour as he had retained his Russian citizenship. In 1922, within a year of his arrival in the Cavendish, Kapitza published a paper in the Proceedings of the Royal Society on "The Loss of Energy of an α-Ray Beam in its Passage through Matter. Pt. I – Passage through Air and CO_2." He presented a reprint to Rutherford bearing this inscription:

"The author presenting this paper with his most kind regards, would be very happy if this work will convince Professor E. Rutherford in two things.

1. That the α-particle has no energy after the end of his range.
2. That the author came to the Cavendish Laboratory for scientifical work and not for communistical propaganda."

Kapitza has recorded* that Rutherford refused to accept the reprint, but that he handed him another which he had brought with him.** Apparently, Rutherford was so convinced.

Kapitza's tremendous energy, drive and self-confidence appealed to Rutherford, as did his voracious appetite for understanding of physical science. This insistent drive to know more led to his founding a discussion club, which met regularly to discuss the major advances and problems

* P. L. Kapitza, loc. cit.
** I found the inscribed reprint when searching for Rutherford papers in the Mond Laboratory – M.L.O.

in physics. At first, Kapitza received his income from the Russian purchasing office in London. Later through Rutherford, Kapitza's work was financed by temporary grants from D.S.I.R.

In April 1930, Kapitza wrote to Rutherford pointing out that he had been working on strong magnetic fields in the Cavendish for eight years. He asked that his position be made more secure through some definite, continuing appointment, which would enable him to expand his work and go ahead without continual worry about the future. In a letter to Rutherford he said that he had received offers from another place, which he did not specify, which was prepared to take over the whole of the equipment of his Magnetic Laboratory at a fair price, but that he would prefer to stay in Cambridge, with Rutherford, to whom he owed so much, if satisfactory arrangements could be made. It seems that this letter precipitated moves which led to Kapitza's appointment to a Royal Society Professorship in 1933, and to the provision of a grant to build the Mond Laboratory for his work. The new laboratory was built beside the Cavendish, on the site of the old electrical substation. It was designed by Kapitza, with much help from Cockcroft, the architect being H. C. Hughes. Eric Gill was commissioned to carve a plaque of Rutherford for the wall of the small, round entrance hall, and to do a carving on the outer wall of light coloured brick, beside the doorway.

Eric Gill turned up in a brown monk's habit, and chipped the brickwork standing on a platform screened by a tarpaulin, so that the work could not be seen till it was complete. Most of us did not know that the carving was to be a formal representation of Kapitza's pet name for Rutherford, the "Crocodile", because he was "the dragon of science". Chadwick tells me that Kapitza told him soon after he joined the Cavendish that, when discussing his work with Rutherford, he was always afraid of having his head snapped off, as by a crocodile. Another reason given for Kapitza's pet name for Rutherford was that, like the crocodile in "Peter Pan", which had swallowed an alarm clock giving advance knowledge of its approach, so Rutherford's voice was heard long before he was seen. Gill's carving met with general approval when unveiled, and it remains a striking piece of work, but the plaque of Rutherford in profile excited shocked dismay among some of his colleagues. Aston, in particular, an extreme conservative, was deeply upset, and tried to have it removed or modified to give the nose a less Jewish appearance, while some of the younger members of the Laboratory talked of hacking it to pieces secretly, at night. Rutherford himself was indifferent, though he did say if he looked like that his name should be "Ruthermond"! Hughes and Kapitza were indignant at the lack of appreciation of the art style and the demand for a photographic representation. The remainder of the story of the carving is best told by reproduction of some letters:

Kapitza to Gill

21st March, 1933

"Dear Gill,
I am sure you would appreciate it if you knew all the fighting I have had lately over your carving. Apparently it irritated some of the most important people in the University so much that they requested that it should be removed. There were big discussions and I had to fight hard and give lectures on Modern Art and its meanings and explain such elementary things as the difference between a photographer and an artist, I do not think I have succeeded in changing their minds, but I think I have succeeded in saving the piece of art, which I appreciate very much.

Rutherford, who found himself in an awkward position, as without his authority nothing could be done and he candidly admits that he is no judge of Art, suggested that the judgment should be left to one of his most famous pupils – Professor Niels Bohr of Copenhagen – who is a lover of modern art. A photograph of the carving was taken and sent to him, and with the only reservation that he has not seen the actual carving himself, but judging by the photograph, he thinks it to be 'a very powerful and thoughtful piece of work'.

Everything is now all right I hope, but I am still surprised to see the extremely formal approach to art existing among most of the people in this country. I had not actually experienced this narrow-mindedness before, but you probably meet with it often. I see they are going to make a fuss about your work on the B.B.C., and I very much sympathise with you for being attacked through being an individualist in your work. ...."

Gill to Kapitza

> "Pigotts, North Dean,
> High Wycombe
> 22.3.33.

Dear Kapitza,

We had a visit from Hughes last week and he told us about the fracas over the Rutherford portrait. I am extremely sorry about it – especially, indeed practically only, because it has been such a nuisance for you. I am very grateful indeed for your championship. Hughes told me that it was all because some people, infected by the Hitler anti-Jew stunt, thought I'd given Rutherford a Jew's nose. Of course that's all nonsense. As I told Hughes, the striking feature of the Jew nose is not its bridge but its *beak*. A prominent bridge is rather Roman

94

than Jewish, and these here classical people ought to have been pleased. What a lot of frightful balls it all is.

I am also very sorry to have been the cause of Lord Rutherford having such a rotten time. Please convey to him my sincere apologies and regrets. The B.B.C. fuss is over, I hear. The old idiot who thought the sculpture was indecent has been snubbed in the H. of C. – so a reporter who rang up said.

I look forward to seeing you again soon. I'm coming down to C. to do that inscription on the base of that great fat vase outside the Senate House soon – as soon as we've finished on the L.M.S. hotel at Morecambe. I hope Mrs. Anna is well and the boys.

Yours ever,
Eric G."

Kapitza to Bohr

10th March, 1933.

"Professor Niels Bohr, F.R.S.,
Blegdamsvej, 15,
Kobenhavn, Ø,
Denmark.

Dear Professor Bohr,

I am writing to you at the suggestion of Lord Rutherford to find out your views on the following matter:

As you know, we have just built here a new laboratory with a grant made by the Royal Society, the building has just been opened, and is called the Royal Society Mond Laboratory. You will find the details of the new laboratory in the booklet issued at the opening which I am sending under separate cover. The possibility of my being able to bring to life my experiments with strong magnetic fields has been due entirely to the support of Rutherford, and to acknowledge the great interest he has taken in our work, I asked an artist to make a carving of him which has been let into the wall of the entrance hall of the laboratory. As you will see from the picture of the laboratory, it is a modern building, and I thought it appropriate to ask an artist of the modern school to do the carving. I chose Eric Gill, since he and Epstein are the two leading sculptors of the modern school in this country.

From the enclosed photograph you will see how he chose to represent Rutherford. It is a fine bit of carving, but a number of people do not approve of it. There are two opinions on the carving – firstly the 'conservative' people consider that there is no likeness whatever to Rutherford, and that it is an insult to him, and request its removal; the others, with whom I agree, think that in order to get a complete likeness of a man there exist such methods as photography and taking of masks, but in modern art the idea is to produce a creation of the artist inspired by the model. Eric Gill, when he was told that the carving was not considered to be a good likeness, told the story of how when Lorenzo de Medici complained that Michael Angelo's portrait of him was not like him, Michael Angelo replied: "It will be like you in a hundred years' time'. Actually Gill thinks he has made the portrait too like and would have liked to simplify it still further.

I personally take the following attitude: that this portrait is meant to honour Lord Rutherford, and only at his personal desire would I be prepared to remove it. Lord Rutherford on being approached by the 'conservative' people, speaking to me, said that he does not understand anything about Art, and is even unable to judge the likeness, although he finds the nose in the portrait too pronounced and more of an Assyrian type. He fails in any case to see any offence in the portrait, and said to me, 'You had better write and ask Bohr's view

– he knows me well, and also takes a great interest in modern art – I should like to know what he thinks".

Well, I am sorry to trouble you, but would like to ask you for your Solomon's judgement.

Accept our most kind regards to yourself and Mrs. Bohr.

Yours sincerely...."

Bohr to Kapitza
"Universitets Institut for   Blegdamsvej, 15,
Teoretisk Fysik   Kobenhavn, Ø
                                                March 15th, 1933.

Dear Kapitza,

It is indeed a very difficult if not impossible task your kind letter has put before me. Even if I have not sufficient qualifications to give a proper judgment in such matters, I have sufficient experience to know, how impossible it is to judge a piece of art from a photograph and without having seen its surroundings. With this reservation, however, the carving of Rutherford looks to me most excellent, being at the same time thoughtful and powerful. I can therefore in no way support the critics of the portrait, and if Rutherford does not object to it and you are satisfied with it, I think that it fulfills its object. I hope that it will remain in its place in many years to come to witness the good work which we all know will be done in your new laboratory. I look forward to see the booklet about the laboratory which I have not yet received, but I am sending these lines off at once, as I am leaving tonight on a skiing trip to get a much needed recreation.

With my best wishes and kindest regards to Mrs. Kapitza and yourself and all common friends in Cambridge from my wife and

Yours sincerely,
N. Bohr"

Kapitza to Bohr

20th March, 1933.

"My dear Professor Bohr,
I thank you very much for your letter which gave me great joy and satisfaction. It was really very good of you to give us your view so promptly.

I quite realize that it is a difficult task to judge a piece of sculpture from a photograph, but in this case I think the photograph gave a correct impression. We hope that soon we shall have the great pleasure of seeing you here in Cambridge, and when you look at the carving your views will not be changed.

Accept my most sincere thanks and best wishes, ..."

Kapitza to Gill

24th June, 1933.

"Dear Gill,
The noise about your carving of Rutherford is gradually quieting down. We had a special meeting of the Buildings Syndicate to consider the question. This had to be done as otherwise the conservative people would have felt themselves completely ignored and it is a little too dangerous as the conservative people are always the most important in this world! Still, we had to make them feel that we were not ignoring their opinion – that would offend them more than anything else!

The Buildings Syndicate definitely decided on my suggestion to do nothing with the carving unless you and Hughes consent. So we decided that when you are here in Cambridge to carve the inscription on the Greek vase we will have a small meeting consisting of yourself, Hughes, myself and two or three members of the Buildings Syndicate (the majority is ours!) which I hope will boil

98

down to a general discussion of Modern Art. Let me know when you are coming, and we shall be very glad if you stay with us while you are doing this job. ...."

Kapitza to Bohr

3rd February, 1934.

"Dear Bohr,

All the troubles with the Rutherford carving are now, I hope, over, and it will be left on the wall.

It is impossible to exaggerate the importance of the role you played in saving its life. I should be glad to acknowledge your support by asking you to accept as a present an author's copy of the original. I have spoken to Eric Gill about it today, and he is quite willing to make one in July when he returns from Palestine.

I propose that the copy should be of the same size and carved in the same stone as the original, provided you do not suggest any alteration to make it suit the surroundings of the place where you propose to keep it. ...."

Bohr to Kapitza

February 9th 1934.

"Dear Kapitza,

I was very happy from your kind letter to learn that your troubles with the beautiful and forceful stone carving of Rutherford are now over, and I am very thankful indeed to you and to the artist for your generous offer to present me with a copy of the carving which I and the whole institute shall greet as a most welcome symbol of what physics and I myself personally owe to our great master. We shall find a fitting place for it in the institute, and I quite agree with your suggestion that the copy should be of the same size and carved in the same stone as the original, as we can always when it is put in place re-mould the surroundings so as to suit it.

With kindest regards to Mrs. Kapitza and yourself from my wife and me with my heartiest thanks."

The Mond Laboratoy was opened in February, 1933. The ceremony was marred only by the unfortunate reaction to Gill's plaque. An invitation to the opening had been sent to Dr. Robert Mond, F.R.S., a son of the great industrial chemist whose bequest of £ 50,000 to the Royal Society enabled the grant for the Mond Laboratory to be made. Mond wrote back from Dinard, where he was living, pointing out that the bequest had been made to enable the Society to meet the expenses of editing an International Catalogue of Scientific Literature, a project halted by the First World War, and that he should have been consulted before the money was used to build a laboratory. Rutherford replied that he was surprised to receive this letter, as he knew that Mond had visited the building and had been in correspondence with Kapitza. He pointed out that:

" .... as a result of a consultation between the University and the Royal Society, it was decided to call the building the Royal Society Mond Laboratory in recognition not only of a distinguished Fellow of the Society, but of a generous benefactor. It was, I think, naturally assumed that any members of Dr. Ludwig Mond's family would be pleased with this tribute to his memory. I can assure you, that if you have not been directly informed of this matter, it is merely inadvertence and not intention, that the whole object of the Royal Society was to do honour to the memory of a benefactor."

He went on to say that both he and Kapitza would appreciate Mond's presence and hoped that he would accept the invitation. I do not know whether Mond decided to be present, but I have found a letter written to him by Kapitza three months before the ungracious letter to Rutherford, telling him that the laboratory was to be named after his father. Kapitza also sent photographs of the building when practically complete, had told him that the opening was planned for early 1933, and invited him to visit the laboratory beforehand. Mond had clearly forgotten all about the proposals. The incident worried Rutherford, who was always gracious and meticulously correct over such matters.

Kapitza had two great achievements to his credit. He had developed methods for producing for short periods of time, magnetic fields of far greater intensity (up to 1 million gauss) than had previously been available, and determined their effects on materials. Realizing that interpretation would be simplified by working at very low temperatures, when the atoms of substances would be virtually at rest, he developed a highly original method for the production of liquid helium to cool his specimens. He did away with the necessity to first cool the helium gas with liquid hydrogen, a dangerous material, by constructing an expansion engine which would operate at temperatures near the absolute zero. With this equipment he made original and important observations. Subsequently, in Eve's words:

"He had been to Russia several times from 1926 onwards, and in 1934 he again went to his native country, partly to attend the Conference held in honour of his great compatriot, the chemist Mendeléeff. Then came the bolt from the blue. A few days before his return to Cambridge, he was informed that he must stay and work in Russia. Now Kapitza without his apparatus or the apparatus without Kapitza was at a standstill. Rutherford wrote to

Stanley Baldwin (29 April 1935): 'Kapitza was commandeered as the Soviet authorities thought he was able to give important help to the electrical industry and they have not found out that they were misinformed.' However that may have been, Rutherford wrote a letter appealing that Kapitza might be allowed, in the interests of science, to return and complete his work. To this the Soviet Government made the sagacious and fair retort that of course England would like to have Kapitza, and that they, for their part, would equally like to have Rutherford in Russia! Since Mahomet could not go to the mountain, the mountain had to go to Mahomet. Negotiations were begun and Professors Adrian and Dirac went to Russia to interview Kapitza and others. Finally the Russian Government bought the apparatus for £30,000 – a fair and proper price – and Cockcroft had the apparatus packed and dispatched to Russia.

Not all this money came to the Cavendish Laboratory, because the British Government, through the Department of Scientific and Industrial Research, had contributed large sums for the generator and other apparatus. It was agreed that the Cavendish would not compete with Kapitza in his field of research, and the money received was devoted to other objects, in the Royal Society Mond Laboratory.

All these worries and troubles about his work and family fell heavily upon Peter Kapitza and Anna his wife, to whom Rutherford wrote most kind and consoling letters. Kapitza accepted the inevitable, settled down to work and determined to do his utmost for the development of Russian science. In 1936 he wrote to Rutherford, with something of Russian fatalism – 'After all we are only small particles of floating matter in a stream which we call Fate. All that we can manage is to deflect slightly our track and keep afloat – the stream governs us!' "

In the magnificent laboratories of the Institute for Physical Problems in Moscow, which Kapitza has directed since its inception, except for a period during the time of Stalin, he has kept alive the spirit of Rutherford. On innumerable occasions he has given lectures and written articles in which Rutherford is the example of greatness in a man of science, and his method of working that which leads most directly to the uncovering of the fascinating properties of matter and space. In August, 1971, Kapitza is to preside at a Colloquium in Moscow, to commemorate the centenary of Rutherford's birth. He acknowledges always the inspiration of working in Rutherford's laboratory, and the immense value he places upon the friendship of so great a man.

REFERENCES

1 P.L. Kapitza "Recollections of Lord Rutherford", Proc. Roy. Soc., vol. A 294, p. 123 (1966).

CHAPTER 8

Working with Rutherford

During my first five years in the Cavendish I worked on some properties of positive ions and on the separation of isotopes by electromagnetic methods. For some time I enjoyed the co-operation of P.B. Moon in what proved to be interesting investigations. R. M. Chaudhri also worked with me. This work involved the production and acceleration of various kinds of ion.

Immediately after the first observations by Cockcroft and Walton, while my wife and I were spending the week-end with the Rutherfords at their cottage, Celyn, at Nant Gwynant, in North Wales, Rutherford told me that he wanted to exploit the new technique as fully as possible in the Cavendish. He suggested that I give up my work with positive ions and use my experience in collaborating with him to set up a second accelerating system. Naturally, I accepted eagerly the privilege of such an arrangement. We decided to aim for greater accuracy in measurement of the energies of the products of these transformations. So I designed and constructed a simple version of the Cockcroft-Walton apparatus, for a maximum energy of 200 keV, and with an improved form of canal-ray tube, giving 100 microamperes or more of protons. This equipment was set up in the room next to that in which Rutherford and Chadwick had done most of their work on artificial disintegration with alpha-particles. Because of the low ceiling, it was necessary to use a horizontal accelerating tube. A brick wall was erected to separate the beam end of the equipment from the high voltage area. This served to reduce greatly the intensity of X-rays in the observing region, and gave us plenty of room for setting up our measuring apparatus. At various times there worked with us A. H. Kempton, Miss Reinet Maasdorp, B. B. Kinsey and Dr. P. Harteck. I have already remarked that Kempton wrote witty songs for the annual Cavendish Dinner; Miss Maasdorp was from Rhodesia, a cheerful soul whose politics were of the extreme left; Kinsey in voice and manner, was a character straight from Wodehouse; while Harteck, an Austrian physical chemist who had been trained in Berlin, was a very large and handsome man with incredible physical strength. All were excellent scientists.

We used magnetic analysis of our beam to ensure that we knew both the kind of bombarding particle we were using, and its precise energy. We were fortunate to have the help of Rutherford's personal assistant, George Crowe, who was very skilled in the splitting of mica to give absorbers of accurately known air-range equivalent, and in mounting these as windows opposite our targets, or as stepped absorbers for measuring the energies of emitted particles. He also prepared alpha-particle sources of polonium and thorium C^1, the particle energies of which were known accurately, to insert in place of our targets for calibration of the equipment. His ability at all laboratory procedures, and his cheerful personality, made working with him a real pleasure.

Initially, like Cockcroft and Walton, we used a scintillation screen to observe the products of transformations. Here, the long experience of Rutherford and Crowe proved of immense value. However, this soon gave way to the electronic techniques of Wynn-Williams and Lewis. Particles were registered as sideways deflections of a spot of light reflected from the mirror of a moving iron oscillograph, of French manufacture, on a moving strip of photographic paper. This was developed and fixed, and then examined by eye to count the number of particles per unit time producing a given ionization in the detecting chamber, i.e., a given deflection of the spot of light. The speed of the mechanical oscillograph limited recording rates to about fifty per second for complete resolution and accurate measurement of amplitude.

Rutherford's participation in the experiments was limited to discussion about what to do next, and deep interest in the results. He gave us a completely free hand in the design of experiments and running of the equipment, but he kept us on our toes all the time. Like all Cavendish equipment up to that time, ours was hastily assembled from whatever bits and pieces were available, so that it often gave trouble. Rutherford was very irritated by delays of this kind, but was singularly uninterested in finding the money to buy more reliable components. However, he was extremely pleased when things went well, giving us a triumphant feeling of something accomplished.

Usually, he came to see us twice each day, late in the morning and shortly before six o'clock in the evening. Occasionally, if something exciting was happening, he would turn up at other times. This was when something was almost bound to go wrong. With Rutherford looking over our shoulders, impatiently awaiting the outcome of an observation, the operator tended to make silly mistakes. On two occasions, Rutherford himself, whose hands tended to shake, pushed something through the mica window through which the products of transformation emerged, letting air rush into the apparatus and creating panic till we had the oil pumps cooled down and everything shut off. He was humbly apologetic, but disappeared for hours, or even days, while we cleaned up the mess and got going again.

If Rutherford appeared just at the end of a run, he insisted that the record be developed as rapidly as possible, barely allowed it to be dipped in the fixing bath, and sat at the table in the next room, dripping fixing solution upon our papers and his own clothes, as he examined the tracing. His pipe dribbled ash all over the wet and sticky photographic paper. He damaged it irreparably with the stump of a pencil from his pocket, with which he attempted to mark the soft, messy material. Searching impatiently for the interesting parts of the long record, he pulled it from the coil in Crowe's hands to fall to the dirty stone floor, often trampling on it as he got up in the end. We had then to do our best to finish fixing, washing and drying the paper strips, often damaged beyond repair. When it was possible, we concealed records from him till they had been properly processed and measured up by us, but this was impossible when he was present while the record was being taken. Once, at the end of a particularly heavy day, when the experiments had gone well, we decided to postpone development till next morning when we were fresh and we could handle the long strip in new developer and fixer without damage. Just as we were leaving, Rutherford came in. He became extremely angry when he heard what we had decided, and insisted that we develop the film at once.

"I can't understand it," he thundered. "Here you have exciting results and you are too damned lazy to look at them tonight".

We did our best, but the developer was almost exhausted, and the fixing bath yellowed with use. The result was a messy record which even Rutherford could not interpret. In the end, he went off, muttering to himself that he did not know why he was blessed with such a group of incompetent colleagues. After dinner that night, he telephoned me at home:

"Er! Er! Is that you Oliphant? I'm er, er, sorry to have

107

been so bad tempered tonight. Would you call in to see me at Newnham Cottage as you go to the Laboratory in the morning?"

Next day he was even more contrite. "Mary says I've ruined my suit. Did you manage to salvage the record?"

He drove us mercilessly, but we loved him for it.

In 1933, G. N. Lewis, from Berkeley, visited the Laboratory. He presented Rutherford with about 0.5 cc of almost pure heavy water, which he had concentrated electrolytically. It was sealed in three tiny glass ampoules. After much discussion, I reacted one of these with a film of potassium deposited on the walls of an evacuated glass bulb, releasing a few cubic centimetres of deuterium. Meanwhile, I asked my colleagues to try the effect of mixing hydrogen with a large excess of helium, to see whether such a mixture gave a reasonable beam of protons when used in the canal-ray tube of our apparatus. We were pleased to find that a mixture of five parts of helium with one part of hydrogen gave precisely the same proton beam as pure hydrogen. We also arranged to collect the gas from our pumping system, and to purify it by freezing out all components other than helium and hydrogen, in a glass trap immersed in liquid nitrogen boiling under reduced pressure, to obtain as low a temperature as possible. We were surprised when the nitrogen solidified to a white crystalline substance, but the method was effective. We were thus able to use our limited supply of deuterium gas over and over again.

We found that the beam of deuterons produced a copious emission of long range, singly charged particles, which appeared to be protons, whatever target we bombarded. Even a clean steel surface produced these particles after the beam had fallen upon it for a short time. E. O. Lawrence had observed such particles produced by the beam from his cyclotron, and had suggested that they arose from break-up

108

of the deuterons into protons and neutrons, in the nuclear fields of the target material. I did not believe this explanation, because the emission from a given target of steel grew with time, and concluded that deuterium was sticking to the target, so that what was observed was the product of the bombardment of deuterium with deuterons. Accordingly, Harteck prepared small quantities of compounds containing heavy hydrogen, by ionic exchange, the first being heavy ammonium chloride, and we made targets by evaporating a drop of a solution in water, placed on a steel target holder, which was water cooled. Immediately, we observed a very large emission of the long range particles, even at bombarding energies of 20 or 30 kilovolts. Rutherford was excited and encouraged us to go ahead. We made certain that the particles were indeed protons, by measuring their velocity in crossed electric and magnetic fields which we calibrated with polonium alpha-particles. I made up an ionization chamber containing helium at high pressure. When connected with the linear amplifier, and placed near the deuterium target, many neutron recoils were observed. A shorter range group of singly charged particles equal in numbers to the number of protons, was shown to be due, almost certainly to the transformation of the nuclei of two deuterons, which fused together to give an unstable helium nucleus, into a new isotope of hydrogen of mass 3, which we called tritium, and a proton.

It was impressive to experience Rutherford's enthusiasm, and the extraordinary process whereby he calculated, by approximate arithmetic, the range-energy relationship of tritium nuclei from the known range-energy curves for alpha-particles and protons. He was so impatient that he kept making slips in his argument. We showed that the momentum relationship was in accord with our assumption, and obtained a value for the atomic mass of tritium very close to that now accepted.

With great patience, instructed by Crowe, I managed to split a sheet of mica, a few square centimetres in area, which showed vivid interference colours, and had a stopping power equivalent to only 1.5 mm of air. Crowe prepared a fine-meshed grid of brass to support this mica, and succeeded in preparing a thin window which withstood atmospheric pressure. This enabled us to look for very short-range particles from our target. We found a group of particles which clearly carried a double charge and appeared to be alpha-particles, in numbers equal to the protons and tritons. This observation produced consternation among us. The equality of fluxes suggested that all three groups of charged particles originated in the same process. Rutherford produced hypothesis after hypothesis, going back to the records again and again, and doing abortive arithmetic throughout the afternoon. Finally, we gave up and went home to think about it.

I went all over the afternoon's work again, telephoned Cockcroft who had no new ideas to offer, and went to bed tired out. At 3.0 a.m. the telephone rang. Fearing bad news, for a call at that time is always ominous, my wife, who wakens instantly, answered it and came back to tell me that "the Professor" wanted to speak to me. Still drugged with sleep, I heard an apologetic voice express sorrow for waking me, then excitedly say:

"I've got it. Those short-range particles are helium of mass three."

Shocked into attention, I asked on what possible grounds could he conclude that this was so, as no possible combination of twice two could give two particles of mass three and one of mass unity. Rutherford roared:

"Reasons! Reasons! I feel it in my water!"

He then told me that he believed the helium particle of mass 3 to be the companion of a neutron, produced in an alternative reaction which just happened to occur with the

110

same probability as the reaction producing protons and tritons.

I went back to bed, but not to sleep. I called in to see Rutherford at Newnham Cottage after breakfast, and went through his approximate calculations with him. We agreed that the way to clinch the conclusion was to measure, as accurately as we could, the range of the doubly charged group of particles, and the energy of the neutrons. I went through our records from the helium pressure chamber, measuring the amplitudes of the most energetic of the helium recoils, and obtaining a maximum neutron energy of about 2 million electron-volts, while my colleagues estimated more accurately the range of the short group. Of course, Rutherford was right. By the end of the morning we had satisfied ourselves that an alternative reaction of two deuterons, produced a neutron and a helium particle of mass 3, the energy released being close to that in the other reaction. The mass of helium three worked out to be a little less than that of tritium.

We all shared Rutherford's excitement. We had found two new isotopes and measured their masses, and we understood the remarkable deuterium reactions. I wrote a note describing our work that evening. This was pencilled all over by Rutherford in the morning, retyped and sent off to 'Nature'. Only in the war was I to experience such a hectic few days of work, but at no other time have I felt the same sense of accomplishment, nor such comradeship as Rutherford radiated that day.

Writing of Rutherford[1], Academician P. L. Kapitza said of his apparent gift of knowledge reached by abnormal methods:

"Many people say that Rutherford possessed an exceptional intuition – as if he felt how an experiment was to be carried out and what was to be searched for. Intuition is

111

usually meant to be some unconscious process – this is
something that cannot be explained and which leads sub-
consciously to the right solution. I personally think that
this may in part be true, but that at any rate this is grossly
oversimplified. An ordinary reader has not the slightest
idea about how hard every scientist works. A layman gets
to know only that part of scientific work which leads to
definite results. Observing Rutherford closely, one could
see what an enormous amount of work he was doing. His
energy and enthusiasm were inexhaustible. He was working and searching for something new all the time. He
published and let his colleagues only know of studies
that led to definite results, but such studies constitute
hardly more than a small percentage of the enormous
amount of work he was doing; the rest was not only
unpublished but even remained unknown to his disciples.
Sometimes only from casual hints could it be guessed that
he tried to do something but that nothing came of it. He
did not like to speak about his research projects and rather
spoke only of what was already performed and yielded
results."

The Berkeley group had given the name "deuton" to the
ions of deuterium. Rutherford disliked this intensely,
feeling that it was too close to neutron, and a "bastard word".
He consulted with his classical colleagues in Trinity about
an alternative, and I know that he wrote to others. As a
result, he proposed that "diplogen" be the heavier isotope
of hydrogen, and "diplon" the nucleus. We wrote several
papers in which these names were used, but he was unsuccessful in his attempt to change the American nomen-
clature. The only concession made to his campaign was to
recognize the possible confusion of deuton with neutron,
and to insert an extra syllable, making it deuteron. However, in the end Rutherford, who had named the particles

112

and radiation emitted by radioactive substances, accepted the decision. He never referred to the problem again.

Rutherford was fascinated by the transformation of boron of mass 11 into three alpha-particles, following capture of a proton. He spent many hours, night after night, puzzling over the continuous distribution of alpha-particle energies which we observed. We repeated the measurements over and over again, but could not make them fit any of the numerous hypotheses which he produced, most of them involving the assumption that emission of the first alpha-particle left behind an excited and oriented nucleus of beryllium of mass 8. He was very pigheaded about this, and wasted much of our time, and his own, over it. Strangely enough, when we found another reaction in which three particles were emitted – lithium of mass 7 breaking into two alpha-particles and a neutron when bombarded with deuterons – his interest revived and he did much more arithmetic, but he did not demand fruitless repetition of measurements. He felt that the alpha-particle, as such, was a constituent of heavier nuclei, and nuclear reactions which released alpha-particles were therefore of particular interest to him.

It was clear from our initial experiments with the small sample of heavy water from G. N. Lewis, that deuterons were of great interest for experimental work on nuclear disintegration. I cabled Cockcroft, who was on a visit to America, asking him, while with Lawrence in Berkeley, to try to obtain more heavy water from G. N. Lewis. Lewis was kind enough to let him have two gallons of water, with two per cent concentration of deuterium, for $ 10. He had trouble convincing the customs on return that the cans contained only water. When he asked Rutherford to refund the ten dollars, Rutherford was angry with him for spending that amount without permission! Dr. Harteck concentrated the deuterium content further by electrolysis. In this way

113

we obtained enough deuterium for all users until heavy water became available commercially from Norway.

Each year, Rutherford gave one or more of the Friday Evening Discourses at the Royal Institution, and for several of these I assisted in the preparation of experimental demonstrations. A few weeks before such a lecture, Crowe would cease to be available for work on the research program, and would devote himself to the drawing of curves and diagrams, and the refurbishing of various pieces of equipment. On the day of the lecture, we would drive to London early, and, with the help of Green, the lecture theatre technician at the Royal Instituion, we would prepare the experiments and exhibits. For his lecture in 1934, Rutherford decided to talk about artificial disintegration, and asked me to help Crowe make a model of our apparatus for exhibition on the lecture bench. After all, if it was not successful as a working model, it would do very well as a demonstration of the kind of equipment we used. I borrowed transformers, rectifiers and some capacitors from an X-ray manufacturing firm in London, so that we did not need to cart up the heavier items, and we set the whole up on the bench. It was touch and go whether we could get it adjusted and operating before the lecture. In case something went wrong, Crowe had a small radioactive source ready to make the counters operate at the right moment – he was an adept at this kind of innocent deception. However, all went well, and Rutherford was able to demonstrate the actual transformation of deuterons by deuterons to the audience which filled the ancient lecture room. Everyone was delighted, Rutherford most of all. The canal-ray tube glowed, the high voltage sizzled, and the loud speaker connected with the counter and amplifier thundered with rapidly increasing speed as the voltage was raised.

Blackett's earlier success in obtaining expansion chamber pictures of the disintegration of nitrogen by alpha-particles, produced a feeling in the Cavendish that the suppositions about the transformations observed by Cockcroft and Walton, and by us, could only be proven beyond doubt by obtaining such photographs and actually seeing the events. P. I. Dee, who was working with C. T. R. Wilson with an expansion chamber, felt this so strongly that he set to work to build a second accelerating tube in Cockcroft and Walton's laboratory. This was arranged to fire a beam of particles onto a target inside the expansion chamber, with thin mica windows permitting the products of a transformation to enter the chamber. This equipment could be connected with the high voltage when Cockcroft and Walton were not operating for any reason. Dee experienced great difficulties in getting the apparatus to function properly, partly because of lack of experience, but mainly because he was impatient to obtain photographs. Finally, he did get very fine pictures of many transformations, but he was mortified to discover that Kirchner, in Germany, was the first to publish such photographs. Dee's greatest triumph was to photograph the tracks of the very short range helium particles of mass 3, from the D.D. reaction. His technique was superb and his photographs were works of art. Rutherford used them whenever he could, to illustrate lectures and to show to visitors. They were such appropriate demonstrations of the very concrete models which he used in thinking about all nuclear processes.

We wished, also, to have definite evidence that the reactions attributed to the lithium isotopes of masses 6 and 7 were correctly assigned. When Rutherford persuaded me to leave my work with positive ions, I was in the middle of setting up a semicircular magnetic focussing mass spectograph, with which to separate the isotopes of potassium, in order to show that it was the relatively rare isotope of mass 40 which was weakly radioactive. The intention was to use thermal ionization on a hot tungsten surface as the source

115

of ions. It was the first version of this source which was ruined by distillation of zinc from the German silver which Lincoln had foisted on to me as pure nickel. I thought of making a new source for use with lithium, but an able young research student, E. S. Shire, who had been assigned to me to help with this task, persuaded me that a simpler approach was possible. He worked out that because of the relatively large difference between the masses of lithium isotopes, an extended source of ions could be used and that these could be accelerated through a grid into a velocity selector, with electric and magnetic fields at right angles to one another. He assembled the necessary equipment very rapidly, and was soon able to provide us with targets on which he had deposited some micrograms of partially separated isotopes. When bombarded in our apparatus, these showed conclusively that the assignments of the reactions to each isotope were correct, and at the same time proved that good separation of the isotopes had been achieved. Rutherford was very pleased with this, especially with the speed with which the work had been done by Shire.

DEUTERIUM

In 1933 the Royal Society arranged a discussion on heavy hydrogen[2], the atomic and nuclear properties of which were becoming clear. Rutherford opened the discussion with a short account of its discovery and of those properties which had been published. Other speakers were Sidgwick, Aston, Harteck, Fowler, Polanyi, Rideal, Bell, Bernal, Jevons and Soddy. All speakers but Soddy spoke of deuterium, or heavy hydrogen, as an isotope of hydrogen. However, Soddy, who coined the word "isotope", objected strenuously to this "misuse" of his term:

116

".... Further, it has been forgotten that this marked difference of chemical character that has been discovered for heavy hydrogen entirely destroys the basis of the prediction. .... I have never given a place in the periodic table to this element at all, and therefore regard the expression 'hydrogen isotope' as doubly a misnomer. It may prove that it is even easier to synthesize heavy hydrogen artificially than to disrupt the light elements. .... Heavy hydrogen bids fair, I think, to be one of the great discoveries of the century. I hope it may prove valuable not only in smashing up a few atoms, but even more so in smashing some of the physical theories of the present day about the whole of them!"

This printed version of Soddy's remarks does not convey their fiery nature nor their bitter satire. He was very angry. In summing up, Rutherford, with tact and gentleness said:

"Before closing the discussion, I am sure you would like me to say a word on the points raised by Professor Soddy in his communication. As you all know, Professor Soddy was the discoverer of isotopes in the radioactive bodies and coined this name because (some of) the radioactive elements appeared to occupy the same place in the periodic table, and to be inseparable by chemical methods. Much water has flowed under the bridge since he made that discovery, and we now speak of the isotopes of an element not as inseparable bodies, but as consisting of atoms which have the same nuclear charge but different masses. .... The name is now given to the atoms of heavy hydrogen which can be readily separated from ordinary hydrogen and shows some very distinctive properties. .... I hope that I have been able to convince Professor Soddy that in using the word isotope for heavy hydrogen we are not contradicting the essential ideas involved in his first use of the word."

117

REFERENCES

1 P. L. Kapitza Collected papers, vol. 3. Pergamon Press: Oxford (1964–1967).
2 Proc. Roy. Soc., vol. A 144, p. 1 (1934).

CHAPTER 9

Home, Holidays, Politics

LADY RUTHERFORD

The Rutherfords lived at Newnham Cottage, an old house with a fine garden, in Queen's Road. Normally, Rutherford walked to and from the Cavendish, and he was close to his College, Trinity, where he dined on Sundays. A relative of Lady Rutherford, Miss de Renzi, lived with them when we arrived, doing some secretarial work for Rutherford and serving often as his chauffeuse.

Lady Rutherford was a keen, but rather erratic gardener. Her knowledge of plants and gardens was great. She was quick to correct any mispronunciation of the botanical names of trees or shrubs, the flowering and growth characteristics, leaves and autumn colouring of which she could describe in detail. But, she was never satisfied, wanting to make changes in layout, introduce new shrubs and plants or cut out or prune drastically what she had admired greatly shortly before. There was a magnificent old walnut tree in the lawn beside the house. She decided that it was shading some more precious plants. Her part-time gardener was elderly and plump, and unable or unwilling to climb the very tall tree. With the excuse that it was dangerous and might shed a branch onto visitors or her grandchildren, she persuaded some of the research students to saw off unwanted limbs on a Saturday. I remember that Wynn-Williams was one of the party, but I cannot recollect who

119

else took part. The ladder available reached only part way up the trunk, and it was necessary to clamber the remainder of the way. Of course, Lady Rutherford wanted the least accessible branches removed, and she insisted that they be cut first from underneath to ensure that no tearing of the bark took place. The ropes at our disposal were thin clotheslines. To sit astride a branch some eight or nine inches in diameter, and cut it from below and then from above with a blunt and unsuitable saw, was not easy. Moreover, when the large and heavy outer part fell, the remaining portion of the branch, relieved of its load, sprang smartly back. It was only by a miracle that I did not fall twenty feet to the ground when this happened, unexpectedly, the first time. Lady Rutherford, as director of operations, shouted contradictory instructions. We never managed to do just what she wished, and she complained bitterly when a branch fell on to a flower bed or dug a hole in the turf.

One autumn, she constructed an elaborate rock garden and stocked it with innumerable alpine plants and exotic dwarfs. She then went off to New Zealand for the winter, arriving back late one evening in the spring, when some of her cherished rock plants should be in flower. Her first action when she reached Newnham Cottage was to go outside to see these with the aid of a torch and matches! Fortunately for those whom she roped in to help with the never-ending task of weeding the rock garden, her interest waned as rapidly as it had grown.

Rutherford was a large man, and since he was talkative and did not pay attention to what he was doing, he was apt to spill tea or food, which settled upon his waistcoat. When this happened, Lady Rutherford would say loudly:

"Ern, you're dribbling!"

He was always apologetic, made a half-hearted attempt to wipe his waistcoat, and promptly repeated the performance.

Rutherford demonstrates the deuterium reactions, Royal Institution. 1934.
Lady Rutherford in front row on left. G.R. Crowe stooping, and M.L.O. standing in front of bench.
W.H. Bragg to right of M.L.O., in front row.

After breakfast at Newnham Cottage on a sunny day

Rutherford and Lady Rutherford at Garden Party

Miss de Renzi and Rutherford, 1931

Of Lady Rutherford, Niels Bohr wrote:[1]

"In later years, it was each time to me the greatest source of renewed encouragement to visit him in his home in Cambridge, where, in spite of never-ceasing work and an even heavier burden of duties, he shared so quiet and simple a life with the companion who, always in contact with what was deepest in his character, from early days stood by him in every joy and sorrow."

Lady Rutherford was a blunt, down to earth woman, round of face and dumpy of figure, but quick of movement. She read widely and possessed an inexhaustible store of knowledge of nature. Possibly because she came from the South Island of New Zealand, she loved Switzerland, especially in spring when the alpine wild flowers followed the snow. She played the piano well, and was an inveterate listener to the B.B.C. broadcasts of concerts of classical music. Placid of nature most of the time, she occasionally displayed an impulse to go abroad, visit New Zealand, redecorate Newnham Cottage, or make sweeping changes in the garden, and then nothing could restrain her. There was no outward display of affection between her and Rutherford, but she cared deeply for him, and for her grandchildren. Her relationship with her daughter, the only child, was not easy, and she was often critical of the husband, Ralph Fowler. It was she who, for most of his life, acted as Rutherford's secretary at home, and it is to her that we owe the wonderfully complete collection of his letters and papers.

Early in December, 1930, I was asked by Lady Rutherford whether I could lengthen the legs of her daughter's bed. Eileen was expecting her fourth child, and it was decided that it should be born at home. It would be convenient if the bed could be raised to approximately the height of a hospital bed. I went round to the Fowler's home, Cromwell

House, and was able to fix the necessary pieces of wood, helped in the process by the two elder children, and hindered considerably by contradictory advice from Lady Rutherford and Ralph Fowler. Lady Rutherford was somewhat concerned for her daughter, and apt to be impatient with both Fowler and me.

All went well with the birth of the fourth child, a daughter. Eileen's sudden death on 23rd December, from a thrombosis, was unexpected and a great blow to her parents and her husband. Lady Rutherford was away in New Zealand, but on her return she did all within her power to help with the grandchildren. In her cables home she persuaded Rutherford to go to "Celyn" in the new year. I accompanied him, Miss de Renzi looking after the house-keeping, etc. He was much shaken by the loss of his only child, and accepted readily many acts of care and affection from Miss de Renzi and me which normally would have irritated him. There was a greater shakiness in his hand-writing, and he tired more easily when walking.

Rutherford was very fond of his grandchildren, and proud of them. Like most elderly men, he could tolerate their presence, and the noise they made, for short periods only, but he liked to see them often.

The Rutherfords occupied separate bedrooms, both at Newnham Cottage and when at their country cottages. There were no overt acts of affection between them. Yet they were devoted to one another. Lady Rutherford under-stood little or nothing of her husband's work, but she was very proud of the honours which came to him and reacted violently to any criticism. She treated him in many ways as she would a child, despite the many years of marriage, still attempting to correct his faults when eating, for instance. I never heard him reply impatiently to her, as would most men when treated in this way. On the rare occasions when Rutherford had a cold or influenza, she nursed him with loving care. She seldom seemed to suffer from such complaints, her only concession to the ordinary ills of the body being periodic bouts of dieting to reduce her weight.

For several years until about 1936, the Rutherfords had living with them Miss Eileen de Renzi (known always as Bay de Renzi), whose mother, a nurse in London, was related to Lady Rutherford. She was in her thirties when we knew her, a mercurial mixture of Irish and Latin ancestry. Whereas Lady Rutherford was cool, competent, and never demonstrative, Miss de Renzi's great affection for Rutherford was shown in countless ways, and he obviously enjoyed being fussed over at times.

In the early days of marriage, in Montreal and Manchester, the Rutherfords were not well off and Lady Rutherford had developed an inherent carefulness about money. This, and her abrupt manner, were not appreciated by servants, who seldom remained long in their employment. On one occasion Lady Rutherford, being about to leave on a trip to New Zealand, was persuaded by Miss de Renzi to engage a man and wife as butler and cook-housekeeper. The presence of the man, fussing about the house and waiting at meals, pleased Miss de Renzi, but irritated Rutherford, especially at breakfast when he was apt to be taciturn, a mood exacerbated by the feeling that he was never alone. The arrangement did not survive Lady Rutherford's return.

The Rutherfords and her many friends were upset when suddenly Bay left Cambridge, for all had grown very fond of her.

Rutherford did not share his wife's love of music. He soon moved to his study to read or write while she played or listened to a broadcast concert. I do not think that he had any appreciation of music. When he burst into song occasionally, it was usually an off-key version of "Onward Christian Soldiers" rendered with great gusto. He appeared to like the loud military bands associated with formal occassions.

123

The Rutherfords liked to get away from Cambridge for part at least of each of the University vacations. While in Manchester they had developed a love of North Wales, the rugged open country, with its clean air, contrasting with their surroundings in the city. They had rented a cottage on the hillside above the highroad between Bettws-y-Coed and Beddgelert, in the valley of Nant Gwynant. The white-washed cottage, with thick stone walls and floors, appeared to have been made by piercing the partitions between two or three very small dwellings of considerable age. Its windows looked out across lush pastures in fields beside the stream which ran through the valley, to the magnificent bare silhouette of Snowdon. Less than a mile towards Beddgelert, the road ran beside a small lake of crystal clear water and stony, bare shores – Llyn Dinas – and crossed the stream in a clump of willows beneath which the cattle came to bathe when the weather was hot. A rough track, the Watkin Path, wound up the branching valley between the cottage and Snowdon, climbing steadily past old slate quarries and above sheer cliffs to the summit of the mountain. My wife and I trudged its many miles several times, enjoying the scramble and the wonderful vistas which it unfolded, but the Rutherfords stuck to less arduous walks. Sheep roamed the hillsides, where outcrops of rock and screes beneath them seemed to cover most of the ground, leaving little for coarse, rough pasture.

In winter the valley was a cold, lonely place, the grass frozen brown and yellow, and clouds scudding across the mountain tops, the summit of Snowdon rarely visible. But it held a strange beauty of its own, and it was easy to appreciate the superstitions which had grown there in the past. In spring, foxgloves in every shade of colour fringed the stone walls and rocks, the grass sprouted green once more, and the lambs gambolled about their mothers. In summer it could be very hot in the valley, but the weather was unpredictable and rain seldom far away.

The stone walls and floors of Celyn seemed always damp, and the bedrooms never warmed. The fine living room was heated with a coal fire, and in cold and damp weather, Rutherford spent most of his time there. He wore a golfing suit with plus-fours and cloth cap. On a warm day, if he went for a walk, he became hot and perspired freely. By the time he demanded a rest, seated on a convenient rock, he was breathless and often irritable.

The Rutherfords had become friendly with a retired Welsh schoolmaster and his wife, the Griffiths, who lived in a cottage overlooking the small lake. Despite his age, Mr. Griffith was very energetic, and could walk for hours over the hills with his well trained dog. I found such walks extremely tiring, but enjoyable because of his conversation about Wales and the Welsh, and particularly about the valley, the dying slate quarries, and folk-lore. Rutherford must have absorbed his fund of stories under other circumstances, for I cannot imagine him on such a walk. On one occasion we had our infant son with us, and like all motherly women, the schoolmaster's wife crowed over him, but always in Welsh. She declared that it was not possible to speak to a baby in barbaric English!

I was at Celyn with Rutherford and Miss de Renzi early in the New Year of 1931, little more than a week after the death of his daughter, when it was announced that he had been created a Baron. He pretended that the new honour was of secondary importance to him, but he could not help showing how he revelled in this recognition of his standing as a man of science. Despite his sadness, one morning he could be heard singing as he dressed. When the heap of letters of congratulations, sent on from Cambridge, arrived each morning, he slit the envelopes with obvious pleasure, passing the contents to Miss de Renzi with some bright quip about the sender. Some he answered at once, but others were kept till he returned to Cambridge.

There was one small store in the valley kept by Mrs. Williams, a well rounded woman with a pleasant Welsh lilt in her voice. Her stock was very limited, fresh bread arriving only once each week, and the butter, produced locally, was excessively salt. For most needs it was necessary to go to Beddgelert by car or by walking the pleasant three to four miles when the weather was good. Rutherford would walk as far as Llyn Dinas, but there he sat to smoke a pipe while we continued on the way. He was fascinated by the remains of an old, very narrow gauge railway track, long disused, which ran beside the road, occasionally tunnelling through rocky outcrops. At one time this toy railway had served a mine and slate quarries, if I remember rightly, but he knew its history intimately.

Celyn was about 250 miles from Cambridge, through country of little interest until beyond Shrewsbury. It was a long and arduous drive. The car was what is known to Americans as a convertible, with hood which could be folded back behind the seats in good weather. There was no heater, or wind-screen wiper, and when in winter it was at times necessary to drive through fog or a snowstorm, with the wind-screen open, it was bitterly cold. Lady Rutherford's passion for fresh air led to driving sometimes with the hood folded back in weather which any ordinary person would avoid. It was amusing to see them both wrapping up for such a drive in woollens, greatcoats, gloves and goggles, and with hot water bottles on the lap of the driver and at the feet of the rugged-up passenger. Almost a day was spent in the journey to or from Celyn, so that it was only used when a stay of at least a week was contemplated.

In 1935 the Rutherfords decided that North Wales was too far from Cambridge, too steep for comfortable walking, Celyn too primitive and too cold for aging bones. After some searching in the southern counties, a spot was found on the Wiltshire downs, in the corner of a large dairy farm, appropriately named "New Zealand", near the tiny village of Upper Chute, not far from Andover. The farmer was willing to sell a few acres, on which were some fine old elms and oaks. At the bottom of the gently sloping area acquired, there was the outline in stone and brick of a small, old building, reputed locally to have once been a chantry, or chapel endowed by its founder for the singing of masses for the repose of his soul. I thought the bricks to be too modern to have formed part of such a chapel, but the legend attracted Lady Rutherford. With the aid of a Cambridge architect, Mr. H. Hughes, who had designed Kapitza's Mond Laboratory and the houses of several of us, she built a simple holiday home, in keeping with the surroundings, and called it Chantry Cottage. Reasonably modern plumbing, including central heating and a bathroom, was installed. To avoid climbing stairs, the Rutherford's bedrooms were on the ground floor, while a large room and a smaller bedroom, beneath the roof, provided for visitors. There was a paraffin stove for cooking, which was not free from troubles, some of which I was called upon to rectify, and lighting was with paraffin lamps and candles. A large brick fireplace at one end of the roomy living room burned wood obtained mostly from the trees below, and gave added warmth, especially in the early morning. My wife and I helped Lady Rutherford to move in and arrange the furniture. Subsequently, we spent many happy holidays there, with the Rutherfords generally, but sometimes on our own.

A settled pattern of life was soon established at Chantry Cottage. Breakfast was a simple meal, at about 8.00 a.m., unless we were leaving early to return to Cambridge. In general, Rutherford was rather taciturn at that time, and there was little conversation other than Lady Rutherford remarking occasionally:

"Ern, you're, dribbling," or: "Ern, you've dropped marmalade down your jacket."

Toast was made at the embers of a roaring fire of twigs and small wood, a stock of which was kept in a wicker basket beside the hearth. The meal over, Rutherford moved to an easy chair near the fire, looked at the "Times" and the "Manchester Guardian" which had been delivered, and then at his mail, which had been sent on from Cambridge. During this process he thawed, and soon he and I would be in the midst of an argument about the Prime Minister, Stanley Baldwin, or some other aspect of politics, where he accused me of getting all my views from "The New States-man". Alternatively, he might discuss some point in a letter which he had received from Niels Bohr, or a book which he was reading on the ancient pathways so prevalent on the ridges of the downs when the valleys were inhospitable places filled with forest and thorns. He became very knowledgeable about the history and archaeology of that part of England, and both he and Lady Rutherford could give fascinating accounts of what they had learnt. There was one of these ancient pathways quite close to the cottage, and the earthworks of British "forts" were not far away, providing interesting objectives for a walk or a short drive.

It was not long after arrival at Chantry Cottage that Lady Rutherford took us outside, asking advice about the development of her garden – advice which she never followed – abruptly correcting my mispronunciation of the botanical name of some tree or plant. Then to the physical labour of digging holes under her supervision, or lopping

128

Celyn

On the Terrace at Celyn. Mrs. Oliphant
and M.L.O.

Snowdon and the Watkin Path

Llyn Dinas from the hill behind Celyn

Hot and irritable after walking

Chantry Cottage

Rutherford weeding at Chantry Cottage

unwanted branches high up in trees. While I was stretched dangerously at full length along a sloping branch, she would direct from the ground which canes of a rampant climbing rose she wished me to remove, not at all perturbed that I was ruining my trousers, or that it was impossible to reach one inch further with the secateurs. Although there was solid chalk beneath a very thin layer of poor soil, she insisted upon planting rhododendrons in holes which I filled with leafmould from the woodland, but since they hate lime, they soon yellowed and died. There was a small pond among the trees where she endeavoured to establish water-loving species which I had to plant, but since it was so overhung by trees and shaded, the only result was that I was covered with mud. Nevertheless, it was great fun endeavouring to help her, and her great botanical knowledge rubbed off, to some extent, upon us.

Later in the morning, if it was reasonably fine, Rutherford would appear and we would cut wood with a cross-cut saw, or chop up the small stuff with axe and tomahawk. He, a New Zealander, and I, an Australian, were no strangers to the cross-cut saw and the axe, so we got on very well. He grunted a lot as he sawed. During our frequent rests he sat on a log and smoked his pipe as he spoke of his boyhood on the farm in New Zealand, telling of his father's sawmill, which cut sleepers for the New Zealand railways under construction, and for export, or of the difficulties of growing flax. When we had done our stint, if there was time before lunch, we would walk up the low hill to see the farmer, with whom he discussed such questions as the greater value of taking a mobile milking shed to the cows, rather than driving the cows to a fixed installation. After lunch, he would doze for a while before the fire, and in the afternoon we might go for a walk or visit a retired petty officer from the Royal Navy, who eked out his pension making novelties of local wood, and who had installed an

129

electric light plant in a shed beside his low-ceilinged cottage.

The evenings were times of relaxation, reading books or discussing world affairs, while Lady Rutherford knitted or sewed, her glasses perched on the tip of her nose. Almost without exception, she played a game of patience before going to bed. Gossip ranged from reminiscences of such events as the ceremonies connected with receipt of the Nobel Prize, or installation in the House of Lords, to methods of controlling the tsetse fly in Africa, or the latest gossip of the royal interest in Mrs. Simpson. Rutherford revelled in pomp and ceremony, especially if he was at the centre, and spoke with gusto of all that had happened. Lady Rutherford intervened occasionally to say:

"Ern, it was not the Duke of Bedford. It was the Earl of Somerset," or some similar contribution to accuracy.

Once, when we were with the Rutherfords at Chantry Cottage, we all went to a military tattoo at Tidworth. It was a fine, balmy evening. The various performances were illuminated by spot lights from above, the performers coming in from a screen of trees at one side of the parade ground. Rutherford was boyishly pleased with the spectacle, the precision of the movements on foot, on motor cycle or on horseback. He stamped his feet in time with the music of the military band, and clapped loudly when an item appealed particularly to him. As we left he remarked generally what a fine entertainment it had been – as indeed it had been – and then to me mischievously:

"That expressed the true spirit of England far better than the nonsense you read in 'The New Statesman'!"

It was to Chantry Cottage that the Rutherfords invited their friends, though all menfolk did not appreciate the tasks they were expected to perform. It brought them great happiness, and Rutherford returned to the Laboratory refreshed by an atmosphere not unlike that of his childhood and youth. To one who knew the completeness of his immersion in his work while in the laboratory, his ability to put it aside and relax utterly while on holiday seemed remarkable. Moreover, he urged his colleagues and students to do likewise, often telling one who was obviously tired to go off for a complete break.

I have heard it said that Lady Rutherford expected him to do too much in the garden there, and that this contributed to the strangulated hernia which led to his death. In my experience, he did nothing which he did not want to do, and I never saw him over-exert himself in the least. He puffed and blew at times, but he did this when he got up from his easy chair to put fresh wood on the fire!

One September we drove to the home of Vernon Boys, who fed us with delicious peaches from his greenhouse. He claimed that this was the only greenhouse in England which had been properly designed. Rutherford was intrigued by the trusses holding up the sloping glass roof which, he asserted mischievously, had redundant members. Boys contested this assertion, using spent matches with which Rutherford had been lighting his pipe to illustrate how each member shared the load. As we drove back Lady Rutherford remarked severely:

"That was quite uncalled for, Ern! You enjoyed his peaches, and you should have kept quiet about his glasshouse."

"But he was quite right Mary, and I knew he was. He enjoyed it as much as I did."

Chadwick has allowed me to quote from a recent letter to me telling of a short motoring holiday spent with Rutherford in 1923 or 1924:

"I don't think that we were away more than a week, if that. R. and I had long talks in the evenings after dinner. During one of these talks R. suddenly said – I say suddenly because it had little connection with our talk on

131

the writing of papers for publication – "You know, Chadwick, I sometimes look back on what I have done and I wonder how on earth I managed to do it all." These may not be his exact words, but they are very near them. His words and manner showed no boasting, some satisfaction at most; what impressed me so much was his modesty, even a degree of humility in looking back on his achievements."

MOTHER

Rutherford wrote regularly to his mother until her death in 1935. In particular, he gave her vivid details of important occasions and ceremonies in which he was involved. It is clear that she was the dominant parent, at any rate with the children, and she played a major part in awakening in them an interest in literature and learning. She abhorred extravagance, and taught them that success came only from hard work. To the end of her long life she retained all her faculties. For most men, the death of the mother is an irreparable loss. Despite her great age, 92 years when she died in 1935, and his own maturity, Rutherford was much upset by her death. Although normally he often dozed when sitting in an easy chair, while awake he was always busily reading or engaged in some other way. Following his mother's death he would sometimes sit staring into the distance, immobile and in deep reverie. He soon recovered, but in my view, never completely. He was to survive his mother by only two years.

POLITICS

The Rutherfords regarded themselves as Liberals. However, as I have indicated already, Rutherford tended

132

to be conservative in most matters. He was a staunch believer in the British Empire, and later in the British Commonwealth of Nations. When science and technology were involved, his concern for people, and for the freedom and health of the search for new knowledge, showed that in these matters he was a true liberal.

In my experience, Rutherford was almost a-political. He accepted men for what they were, irrespective of politics. I never heard him make derogatory remarks about a politician or civil servant, though he would joke about them. When Lord Bledisloe was Governor-General of New Zealand, he referred to him always as "Bloody Slow", but liked him and his company. Nevertheless, he became much disturbed by the growing political unrest in Europe, which was rapidly eroding freedom and threatened the eclipse of democracy. Thus, at a meeting of the Cambridge University branch of the Democratic Front, over which he presided, he said:

"It is a matter of great importance that those who believe in the present type of government should not stand idly by, but see if they can convince the waverers, or those who require convincing, of the great advantage of democratic government, at any rate in this country where we have experienced it so long.

At present there is a great feeling of tension, not only throughout Europe, but in a sense throughout the world. That feeling of tension and fear of war has been a striking mark of the last few years. This arises largely from the fear of the growing power of military aeroplanes with sudden and devastating attacks on defenceless cities, involving the destruction of combatants and non-combatants alike.

I am sure that the greatest possible relief from this fear of war would arise, if say, to-morrow we could ensure that aeroplane warfare could be abolished by consent of all the nations of the world. That would be a great epoch in history, but it may not be possible for a long period. ..... There is no question more important for the future than to see whether we can get some form of international agreement on the limitation of this air weapon which will undoubtedly grow in strength from year to year."

How much more strongly would Rutherford have spoken now, when chemical, biological and nuclear weapons can be delivered anywhere on earth with great accuracy by unmanned rockets?

REFERENCES

1 N. Bohr "Nature", vol. 140, p. 1049 (1937).

CHAPTER 10

Rutherford and Nuclear Energy

In November 1947, ten years after his death, a large gathering was organized by the World Association of Scientific Workers to pay homage to Rutherford. I was invited to be present to speak and to represent the Royal Society. Lady Rutherford, with the grandchildren Peter and Elizabeth Fowler were also invited. Before leaving Birmingham, I received a letter from Lady Rutherford suggesting that I refer in my talk to a letter from Whetham to Rutherford written in July 1903, quoted by Eve in his biography:

".... I am writing an article on radioactivity .... and shall be glad to have your papers before me.

In my first rough draft I mention your playful suggestion that, could a proper detonator be found, it was just conceivable that a wave of atomic disintegration might be started through matter, which would indeed make this old world vanish in smoke.

I don't know if you care to be thus quoted in print, as I do not think you have published your views about the end of the world, but I make it quite clear that it was only a speculation...."

According to Eve, Whetham was referring to a joke of Rutherford's that: "Some fool in a laboratory might blow up the universe unawares." At the meeting, in the presence of the President of France, an array of great men of science including Bohr, Bhabha, Blackett, de Broglie, Frisch, Hevesy, Lise Meitner, G. P. Thomson, H. Urey, sat on a platform beneath a portrait of Rutherford projected onto a large screen, and each spoke shortly, but with great feeling in memory of their master. Some of my remarks were:

"I speak this evening as a pupil of Rutherford who was privileged to work closely with him from 1927 to 1937, and as one who enjoyed his personal friendship.

I speak also as the representative of the Royal Society of London, of which Rutherford was President, and which is glad to be associated with this international tribute to his greatness as a scientist and to his outstanding qualitites as a man.

Those of us who knew and revered Rutherford are very grateful to all who have made possible this gathering, to the World Federation of Scientific Workers, to the French Government, to the College de France and especially to Professor Curie-Joliot, for this opportunity to pay tribute to his memory. I am honoured that I have been asked to take part in it and I thank you warmly.

The present domination of international affairs by the implications of atomic energy emphasizes the practical consequences of Rutherford's work. These aspects will be dealt with by other speakers, especially in the session of tomorrow afternoon.

I wish to devote my present remarks to those human qualities which I believe to have contributed more than any other attribute, to his great influence upon the world of science.

Unlike Newton, Faraday, Maxwell and other great men in British physics, Rutherford worked with and through his colleagues and research students. All his life he was surrounded by young men and through them his influence continues to dominate physical science, not

With grandchildren on the beach

On holiday with Fowler, the grandchildren and friends.

On the sands

Lady Rutherford with her grand-daughter, Elizabeth, and the
President of France, M. Auriol, Paris, 1947

only in the British Commonwealth, but throughout the world. His straightforward, uncompromising approach to scientific truth, his infectious enthusiasm and his boyish manner, were a combination of qualities which called forth all that was good in those who came in contact with him. He referred to the members of his laboratory, old and young, as "the boys", and treated them always as such. He would argue earnestly with the youngest research workers and would often defer to the judgment of his least experienced colleague; yet in the final analysis his word was law, because his uncanny intuition made him almost always right.

The infection of his enthusiasm and the charm of his personality extended his influence beyond the range of his professional contacts. ....

Nuclear physics, which Rutherford himself had largely built, founded upon the discoveries of illustrious French scientists, Becquerel and the Curies, was not a popular branch of physics until it had been romanticised by the development of the engines of nuclear disintegration. Its full implications were not appreciated by all and at times Rutherford found himself severely criticised for producing a type of research physicist initially of little use in tackling the practical problems of industry or of the government services. He recognised, and taught others to recognise, that the fundamental problems of nuclear physics were the growing points of physical science, and they still remain so.

Rutherford's uncanny judgment of what were the prime problems of physics was seldom at fault. In general whatever he did and whatever he gave his pupils to do, led to results of importance, sometimes of extreme importance. But equally well he knew when to stop, when to drop unprofitable investigation and when to postpone a difficult experiment till improved technique made it

137

possible. He advocated always a qualitative approach to a problem so that a simple answer was obtained on which to base a quantitative attack. Thus time was not wasted in building too elaborate apparatus and often the preliminary results, accurate to 10 or 20%, proved adequate for his inspired reasoning.

Rutherford was a good judge of human character, but his verdicts were inevitably generous. If a man was blamed by Rutherford he deserved castigation; if a man was praised by him, his words often needed dilution to arrive at the truth. I never heard him say an unkind thing against anyone, and when, occasionally, his liver or some particularly foolish act by someone in the laboratory, drove him to anger, he was invariably contrite and apologized afterwards. He was a true internationalist; for him national barriers in science just did not exist; his faith in such matters was simple and profound. Rutherford never really believed that the release of atomic energy would prove possible. ....

I think he shied away from any practical application of this field of work. The knowledge of the inmost workings of nature, which it gave, was in many ways to him a sacred subject, not to be profaned by applications with political and industrial implications. For him, scientific investigation was the greatest adventure of mankind. He would be very unhappy to see the present pitiable state of that "Tom Tiddler's ground" of opportunity in which he dug so well.

Rutherford is still strongly alive in the minds and affections of those whom he inspired. In any given set of circumstances we find ourselves asking "what would the professor have done under those circumstances, and what would he have thought of this idea?' So long as we live he will live vividly in our hearts, and if we can do a little to hand on that flaming torch, we shall be content!"

A sequel to my participation in this moving gathering, was that I was unable to obtain a visa to visit the United States for a year or two during the McCarthy period. I discovered through the American Ambassador in Australia that the reason was that the meeting had been communist inspired, and run by a communist dominated body, while the principal organizers, Curie-Joliot and his wife, were known communists!

Sir James Chadwick has pointed out to me that in the first edition of his book, "Radioactivity", published in 1904, of which I possess the copy once owned by A. S. Eve, Rutherford discussed the large total energy emitted in the radioactive changes undergone spontaneously by radium.

"The difference between the energy originally possessed by the matter, which has undergone the change, and the final inactive products which arise, is a measure of the total amount of energy released. There seems to be no reason to suppose that the atomic energy of all the elements is not of a similar order of magnitude .... If it were ever found possible to control at will the rate of disintegration of the radio-elements, an enormous amount of energy could be obtained from a small quantity of matter".

He went on to discuss the maintenance of the heat of the sun and the thermal gradient of the earth through nuclear transformations, and the probability that the age of both could be much greater than the 100-500 million years calculated by Lord Kelvin.

A. S. Eve, in his biography, says that on 7th February, 1916, Rutherford spoke at the New Islington Public Hall on "Radiations from Radium". In the course of this lecture:

"He said that scientists wanted to ascertain how they could release at will the intrinsic energy contained in radium and utilize it for our own purposes..... It had to

139

be borne in mind that in releasing such energy at such a rate as we might desire, it would be possible from one pound of the material to obtain as much energy practically as from one hundred million pounds of coal. Fortunately at the present time we had not found a method of so dealing with these forces, and personally he was very hopeful that we should not discover it until Man was living at peace with his neighbours.'

This lecture, delivered at the height of the First World War, has an ominous, almost prophetic significance today.

At the Leicester meeting of the British Association in 1933, Rutherford recalled that it was in Leicester in 1907 that Kelvin had categorically claimed that the atom was the indestructible unit of matter. After discussing recent work on the disintegration of atoms he said:

"These transformations of the atom are of extraordinary interest to scientists but we cannot control atomic energy to an extent which would be of any value commercially, and I believe we are not likely ever to be able to do so. A lot of nonsense has been talked about transmutation. Our interest in the matter is purely scientific, and the experiments which are being carried out will help us to a better understanding of the structure of matter."

During our work on the nuclear reactions between the nuclei of heavy hydrogen, we found that these could be observed at bombarding energies of less than 20 keV. I wondered whether it might be possible to obtain more energy from such reactions than was necessary to produce them, and with the aid of Crowe built a high voltage canal ray tube in which the deuterium ions passing through the cathode could be absorbed completely in deuterium gas. Rutherford, who had been away while we were doing this, was quite angry that we had wasted our time in this way:

140

"Surely I have explained often enough that the nucleus is a sink, not a source of energy!"

He had. His argument went as follows. The binding energy of a proton or neutron, in a nucleus, is of the order of 6–7 MeV. In order to take a nucleus to pieces, therefore, 6–7 MeV had to be added to it for each proton or neutron removed. He was adamant about what he called "a general rule", though he knew better than anyone that a very large amount of energy was set free in the spontaneous transformation of uranium into lead, and he had speculated that it was the formation of helium by the union of hydrogen atoms at the hot centre of the sun or star which maintained its temperature. In his lectures he made great use of Aston's "packing fraction" curve for the elements, which showed clearly that large amounts of energy should be available if the very light, or the very heavy elements could be transformed into those of medium atomic mass.

Those who did not know Rutherford well could conclude that he seemed to be deliberately obtuse, a rare phenomenon in one whose mind absorbed so rapidly and completely any nuclear information. I believe that he was fearful that his beloved nuclear domain was about to be invaded by infidels who wished to blow it to pieces by exploiting it commercially. Also, he disliked speculation about the practical results which could follow from any discovery, unless there were solid facts to support it. In his address prepared as President of the combined Science Congress in India in 1937, read to the Assembly by Jeans, he spoke of the effectiveness of the neutron in producing nuclear reactions, particularly reactions in which the product nucleus was radioactive:

"For example, a number of these radio-elements are produced when the heaviest two elements, uranium and thorium, are bombarded by slow neutrons. In the case of

141

uranium, as Hahn and Meitner have shown, the radio-active bodies so formed break up in a succession of stages like the natural radioactive bodies, and give rise to a number of transuranic elements of higher atomic number than uranium (92) .... of atomic number 93, 94 and 95".

It is ironic that even as he wrote, Hahn and Strassman were observing that radioactive elements of much lower atomic number were also produced, indicating the fission of the uranium nucleus and the beginning of the age of nuclear weapons and nuclear power.

Much nonsense has been written and said about the early history of nuclear energy. Thus Einstein's relationship between mass and energy, $E = mc^2$, where m is mass, c the velocity of light and E the equivalent energy, is for many the basic truth from which the practical realization of nuclear energy for weapons and for industrial power, has followed. In fact, this achievement rests squarely upon the work of Rutherford, who discovered the nucleus, invented the methods for investigating its properties, and showed that nuclear transformations were accompanied by emission or absorption of energy enormously greater than the energies associated with chemical reactions. Einstein's relation gives a method for calculating energy changes if the initial and final masses of the nuclei involved are known with sufficient accuracy. More often the masses are calculated from the observed energy changes. However, the knowledge of nuclear properties which led to the release of nuclear energy could have developed as far if the theory of relativity had not been born.

In all nuclear processes through which useful energy can be obtained, the total number of nucleons, i.e., of constituent particles of the reacting nuclei, remains unchanged, just as in the burning of a fuel the number of atoms involved is constant. All that happens, in either case, is that the state of combination changes, the large energies associated with nuclear transformations arising from the magnitude of nuclear binding forces.

CHAPTER 11

Directing Research, D.S.I.R., Science and People

DIRECTING RESEARCH

When I became an Assistant Director of Research in the Cavendish, Rutherford sent for me to talk about my duties. He spoke of the problem of finding tasks for research students which were worth doing, and yet within the capacity of the raw recruit to original investigation. He pointed out that an extremely good result in the Tripos or other honours degree examination was not necessarily an indication of research ability. A man who had an idea of his own of what he wished to do should be encouraged to try it out, even though it did not seem very important or even feasible, for one learnt from mistakes as well as successes.

"Watch him and see how he goes about it, and if it looks very doubtful persuade him to try something else."

He went on in this vein for some time. Then suddenly he said:

"I've been talking about how to make a beginning in research. But there is a far more important and difficult decision which must often be made. That is to know when to stop, how to discard a line of work which becomes unprofitable." He told of "dead horses which continue to be flogged", giving examples, a few of them in the Cavendish itself! I was much impressed by his emphasis upon encouragement of any spark of originality:

"Don't forget that many a youngster's ideas may be

144

better than your own, and never resent the greater success of a student."

This generous attitude was apparent in all his papers and lectures, where he was meticulous in attributing ideas and experimental results to others. He did not appreciate those who boasted too much of their own achievements, or that of their laboratories, though at times he himself was not completely free from this fault, especially when speaking of the Cavendish. Dr. Bretscher has recalled for me an occasion when a young man spoke of nuclear reactions about which he had been thinking, as "my reactions". Rutherford's blood pressure rose immediately as he retorted:

"Are you God that you call them *my* reactions?"

Rutherford did not expect spectacular results, though his deep pleasure was evident when they came, but he did expect devotion to research. What is more, he was confident that knowledge of nature was as yet elementary, and that research into any of the phenomena of nature could be rewarding. He often likened science to Tom Tiddler's ground, for wherever one dug with intelligence and energy, no matter how many times it had been dug over before, something interesting was bound to turn up.

D.S.I.R.

For seven years, until his death, Rutherford was Chairman of the Advisory Council of the Department of Scientific and Industrial Research. I often met him at the railway station in Cambridge after a trip to London, and drove him to Newnham Cottage, sometimes in the evening following a meeting of that Council. He always had something to say about the work of the day. On one occasion, if I remember rightly in 1931, he was very quiet when he got into the car, and when I asked whether the day had gone well, he said that he was worried because members of Council had again attacked him for not relating the work of the Cavendish more closely to the industrial needs of the nation. Moreover, he had been accused of producing research workers who were of little or no use when faced with "real" problems. On a later such occasion, in about 1935, when he thought that any misgivings should have been laid to rest through Chadwick's discovery of the neutron and Cockcroft and Walton's demonstration of transformations produced by artificially accelerated particles, he said:

"They have been at me again, implying that I am misusing gifted young men in the Cavendish to transform them into scientists chasing useless knowledge."

Rutherford's spirits soon recovered. He realized, more than most, the importance of the application of scientific knowledge if Britain was to prosper, but he remained convinced that one of the best training grounds for physicists was the sort of fundamental science pursued in the Cavendish. His faith was demonstrated dramatically after his death, when the needs of war found almost all the men whom he had trained leading such practical developments as radar, atomic energy, and operational research.

I remember accompanying Rutherford on a visit to the Forest Products Research Laboratory, at Princes Risborough. He showed an eager interest in all that was going on, though it was all far removed from his own field of work. He asked penetrating questions about the darkening of timber from oak trees which was produced by a fungus, the fruit of which appeared as a very large shell-like growth from the bark, known as the beefsteak fungus. An apparatus for determining the relative wearing qualities of different timbers for heavy duty flooring, in which feet were imitated by swivelling lasts, soled with brake-lining material, which shuffled for ever across a floor which was a mosaic of many timbers, fascinated Rutherford as ingenious and bound to

146

give valuable answers. He sat and talked with the youngest of research workers as he did in the Cavendish, as eager to learn from them as they were to hear what he had to say. Remembering the rape of the magnificent timber stands in his native New Zealand, he was keen to know what steps were being taken to ensure continuity of supplies of desirable species, especially those grown in Britain. He questioned all workers about their links with industry and with the fundamental biology, chemistry and physics which were at the base of their activities.

Following Rutherford's death, Sir Frank Smith, Secretary to D.S.I.R., paid tribute[1] to his work as Chairman of the Advisory Council:

"Lord Rutherford's death is a calamity for the Department of Scientific and Industrial Research. In the seven years during which he has been chairman of the Advisory Council, his influence has made itself felt throughout the Department. His broad sympathies, lively imagination, and deep insight equipped him in a wholly exceptional way to direct and strengthen the links between the Department and industry. It was an article of faith with him that the future of Great Britain depends upon the effective use of science by industry. It was this faith which induced him, a man of the highest attainment in the field of pure scientific research, to devote himself, as he did unreservedly, to our work. The development of the research association movement, now taking place, owes much to his foresight, sympathy and advocacy. Equally stimulating was his influence on the scientific work of the Department. In our counsels he leaves a blank which cannot be filled; and the loss of his unsparing service, his genial personality, and his warm-hearted encouragement, may well fill the stoutest heart with dismay."

In his Norman Lockyer Lecture for 1936, Rutherford spoke on "Science in Development". He said:

"In surveying the great tide of advance in the Physical Sciences during the past forty years, it is not always recognised how much the progress of discovery has been influenced, and indeed in many cases controlled, by the improvement of laboratory technique and by the development of new instruments and methods of measurement. It is not easy for the young investigator to-day to realize the great changes which have taken place in the methods and apparatus of investigation in the life-time of the older generation of scientific workers in Physics, or to evaluate the effects of these changes in assisting the advance of industry.

In assessing the merit of any scientific discovery, it is always of much importance to view it against the background of the knowledge and of the instrumental and technical facilities available at the time of the discovery. For example, it is quite possible in some cases for an elementary student to-day with modern apparatus and technique to repeat with ease and rapidity the observations that led to an important addition to knowledge, say a century ago, although the making of the first discovery may have required not only much originality of outlook and method but possibly also a difficult and laborious investigation with the relatively crude laboratory facilities then at the disposal of the experimenter. ..."

After discussing the great changes which had taken place in the 40 odd years since he began his research work, and giving some examples, he spoke in detail of the development of vacuum techniques and their applications to the manufacture of electric lamps, X-ray tubes and electronic valves, and ended with these words:

"This orderly application of scientific research to industrial ends has undoubtedly been of great material benefit to mankind. These remarkable developments have not led to any serious displacement of labour in older industries, but have rather given new avenues of employment for great numbers of men and women.

During the last few years, there has been much loose and uninformed talk of the possible dangers to the community of the unrestricted development of science and scientific invention. Taking a broad view, I think that it cannot be denied that the progress of scientific knowledge has so far been overwhelmingly beneficial to the welfare of mankind. The particular case of the application of Science I have spoken of to-day is a good illustration of this. It is, of course, true that some of the advances of Science may occasionally be used for ignoble ends, but this is not the fault of the scientific man but rather of the community which fails to control this prostitution of Science. It seems to me that scientific men have shown themselves unduly sensitive to these criticisms although it is a natural reaction in an investigator who is conscious that his only aim in his work has been to add to the sum of human knowledge. It is sometimes suggested that scientific men should be more active in controlling the wrong use of their discoveries. I am doubtful, however, whether even the most imaginative scientific man except in rare cases is able to foresee the ultimate effect of any discovery. It may be, however, that some method of control of the rate of application of new ideas or inventions to industry is desirable in the public interest, in order to prevent too marked a dislocation both of capital and labour. The application of an improved and cheaper method of production in an industry may be inevitable for economic reasons and ultimately for the benefit of the community as a whole, but yet too rapid a change over may result in severe hardship and lead not only to the displacement of skilled labour, but to large losses of capital. This question has been ably discussed by Sir Josiah Stamp in his Presidential Address before the British Association this year, and he has endeavoured to make an estimate of the losses involved by the sudden application of new inventions to industry. In the present state of industry, when progress and change are rapid, it seems to me that it would be an advantage to the State to know the probable changes to be expected in industry before they were actually put into operation. For this reason, it would seem to me desirable for the Government to set up what I may call a 'Prevision Committee' of an advisory nature. The function of this Committee, which would be composed of representatives of business, industry and science, would be to form an estimate of the trend of industry as a whole and the probable effects on our main industries of new ideas and inventions as they arose, and to advise whether any form of control was likely to prove necessary in the public interest. A competent committee of this kind could no doubt have foreseen the coming competition between motor and railway transport, which had such serious effects on the latter, and have advised the Government as to the need of adjustment of competing claims before the difficulties became acute. While all will agree that industry should be alert to take prompt advantage of new methods made possible by the advance of Science, yet it may be important in the public interest to graduate the rate of change to prevent too serious dislocations in the social order. A Committee of this kind would have a difficult and responsible task, but could not fail to be

150

helpful to the Government in advising it of the trend of change for industry in general and to inform it of possible dislocations of industrial life which may suddenly arise from the impact of scientific discovery."

With some slight changes of emphasis these words are even more applicable to the situation today. The advent of nuclear energy, which arose from Rutherford's own work, of the computer and automation, is producing profound changes in the relations between science and technology and the society in which they exist. Serious problems face the world, nationally and internationally. It is to be regretted that Rutherford's wisdom is not available to help find solutions.

CHAPTER 12

The end

I LEAVE CAMBRIDGE

Early in 1936 the Dean of the Faculty of Science in the University of Birmingham, Professor N. Moss, called on Rutherford to ask whether he could assist in finding a man to fill the Poynting Chair of Physics in that University. Rutherford sent him to talk with me. I was reaching the stage where I felt that I wanted a show of my own. Rutherford had told me that he intended to retire at 70, and I could not envisage working in the Cavendish under any other professor. So I told Moss that I was interested and arranged to visit Birminghan to see the laboratory there. It was clear that while my colleagues in the Department of Physics would make a good team with which to work, the equipment and facilities were not very attractive. However, W. N. Haworth, the Professor of Chemistry, who was later to be awarded a Nobel Prize and a knighthood in recognition of his outstanding contributions to chemistry, was most persuasive and reassuring about what could be done.

I wrote to Chadwick who replied in a long and helpful letter which is well summed up by quoting the following passage:

"To me all seems to depend on whether this is the kind of post you want – if you want a university chair and laboratory of your own. If you feel lukewarm about this, then it would be a mistake to go to Birmingham or any other university. If you do want a chair, then I think arrangements can and must be made which should satisfy your obligations to Cambridge and to yourself."

Although he had sent Moss to talk with me, Rutherford was very angry indeed when I told him that I was tempted to go to Birmingham. He grew red in the face and shouted that he was fated to be surrounded by ungrateful colleagues, and much else, ending by:
"Go and be damned to you!"

I had never before been on the receiving end of one of Rutherford's choleric outbursts, though I had heard of them, so left his room greatly upset and worried. Shortly afterwards, he came to my room where I was sitting in despair, and asked hesitantly, could I spare time to talk with him. His apology for his reception of my news was complete, reinforcing my distress at having upset him. He went on to discuss how the work upon which I was engaged could be continued, and what he could do to help me if I did move to Birmingham. In the end, it was agreed that I should accept the appointment, provided that I could take it up in September, 1937. Rutherford proposed me for election to the Royal Society, and it must have been through his influence that I was elected that year.

THE DEATH OF RUTHERFORD

Rutherford suffered from a slight hernia at the umbilicus, for which he wore a truss harness. Normally, it did not appear to worry him. He spent most of September, 1937, at Chantry Cottage, where he was his usual relaxed and cheerful self. He had been preparing the Presidential Address which he was to give to a joint gathering of the

153

Indian Science Congress and the British Association for the Advancement of Science, and had done much reading of material of significance for the occasion. He looked forward to the gathering, for not only would he meet many former students, he would have the opportunity to encourage the pursuit of science in another part of the British Commonwealth of Nations, in which he believed implicitly. As usual, the address was prepared with great care and attention to detail.

What followed is best told by Lady Rutherford, in a letter written from the Evelyn Nursing Home in Trumpington Street, Cambridge, in the late afternoon of Tuesday, 19th October, 1937:

"My dear Mark,

You will have heard from someone of my husband's illness. He was seedy – indigestion – on Thursday, doctor next morning, operated that night, Friday, for strangulated hernia. There was no gangrene and they were very pleased, some paralysis of the gut which they thought was got rid of. On Sat. as well as cd. be expected. On Sunday vomiting all day showed there was serious mischief. That night washed out stomach and put permanent tube in by the mouth to keep siphoning all the time. Since yesterday morning he's had intravenous injection of saline going all the time. Yesterday morning Nourse* and Prof. Ryle, Regius Professor who has been consulting several times a day, decided to get the surgeon down again for a second operation. He is Sir Thos. Dunhill and absolutely first class and charming – a Melbourne man by the way. He talked it over last night after examining Ernest and decided it was no use to operate and practically said that nothing could be done, age etc. were factors. This morning the other two said the same.

* Dr. Nourse was the family physician.

154

Today however at 4 p.m. Nourse said he couldn't see that he was any worse than at 8 a.m. and today he has retained a few oz. more than he has expelled and he has had 6 pints by the vein since 1 p.m. yesterday. He is a wonderful patient and bears his discomforts splendidly, so tired and weary of these interminable days.
There is just a thread of hope!
Love to Rosie.

Yours affectionately
Mary Rutherford.

Dunhill was Ryle's choice, an old friend. Great opinion of his diagnosis as well as his surgery."

John Cockcroft and I had been invited to take part in a celebration of the two-hundredth anniversary of Luigi Galvani's birthday, and the favourable report after the operation led to our leaving for Bologna, Italy, without undue anxiety. However, the thread of hope which Lady Rutherford mentioned was broken later that day, and Rutherford died peacefully on Tuesday, 19th October, 1937, in the evening.

The news of Rutherford's death was telegraphed to us by P. I. Dee, reaching us early in the morning of 20th October. We at once told Bohr, who was at the Conference, and made preparations for immediate return. When the meeting scheduled for that morning assembled, Bohr went to the front, and with faltering voice and tears in his eyes informed the gathering of what had happened.

Bohr went on to give a short address about Rutherford, which was one of the most moving experiences of my life. He spoke from his heart of the debt which science owed so great a man whom he was privileged to call both his master and his friend. It is to be regretted that no direct record*

* The version published in "Nature", vol. 140, p. 752 (1937) is much shortened and deprived of the intensity of Bohr's spoken word.

was made of this great tribute. Cockcroft and I, shocked by the news and grieved that we were away when it happened, returned as rapidly as possible. I found a further letter from Lady Rutherford, who had written at once, giving details of the end. She said that in his last days Rutherford and she renewed the deep affection and love of their youth, and he spoke to her with tenderness and concern for her future. Very near the end he said suddenly to her that he wanted to leave one hundred pounds to Nelson College and asked her to see to it for him.

On Friday, 21st October, before the cremation, Philip Dee, who was very upset, said that he would like to see Rutherford once again, and would I go with him. We went to the mortuary where the body lay, pale and still. After we had left, and a few moments of quietness, we agreed that all that made Rutherford for us had gone, and only a shell remained. I was distressed greatly by this experience.

Rutherford's ashes were laid beneath the nave of Westminster Abbey, near the tomb of Sir Isaac Newton, at a simple but moving ceremony.

Lady Rutherford asked me to go through Rutherford's papers, together with Ralph Fowler, who had other things to do, so that most of the task fell to me. His correspondence was not filed in any order, but thanks to Lady Rutherford's care was extraordinarily complete, from his letters to his mother and his fiancee when first a student in Cambridge, to his last days. Full use was made of these by A. S. Eve, his official biographer.

Among his letters I found one from Professor Pohl, with a single flimsy disc recording part of a lecture which Rutherford had given in Göttingen on 14th December, 1931. I wrote to Professor Pohl asking whether he had recorded the whole lecture, and if so whether he could let me have the remaining discs. By good fortune, he was able to send them to me, and I arranged with Dr. Schoenberg, of the Gramo-

156

phone Company, to have them reproduced in permanent form. The result was excellent, and many albums of the records were distributed to those who wished to hear Rutherford's characteristic voice again.

CONCLUSION

Almost all who knew Rutherford, and have written about him, say that he was the greatest experimental physicist since Faraday. Max Born, whose own contributions to theoretical physics were formidable, said that he was the greatest scientist he had ever known, including even Einstein.

In some ways Rutherford's work was more significant than that of Faraday or Einstein, for whereas he worked with and through a multitude of students and colleagues, and thereby exercised an enormous influence on the world-wide development of physics, Faraday worked alone, and Einstein had few close collaborators. He was a man of far more "out-going" temperament than either, so that his influence extended beyond his physics in the world of science, and reached leaders in industry and government outside.

Rutherford escaped the complexities of religion which afflicted Farady, and Newton also in an earlier age, or the problems of race which worried Einstein, a Continental Jew. Indeed, in all ways except in his science, Rutherford was an exceptionally ordinary man in both appearance and character. Quite naturally, he was friendly with all men and quarrelled with none. He could be moody, irritable, and on very rare occasions angry, but as with most men such deviations from the normal were rare and transient. His success came as much from complete dedication to his work as from his innate ability, so that even the average

157

student was inspired to emulate him. Yet, ordinary as he was, there was something in him which raised him high above others and put him in the company of the greatest of men, and this something earned for him both the profound respect and the deep love of all who came under his influence.

92
Rutherford

86888

DATE DUE

GAYLORD			PRINTED IN U.S.A.